VICTIMS AND NEIGHBORS

VICTIMS AND NEIGHBORS

A Small Town in Nazi Germany

Remembered

FRANCES HENRY

Foreword by Willy Brandt

BERGIN & GARVEY PUBLISHERS, INC.
Massachusetts

Library of Congress Cataloging in Publication Data

Henry, Frances, 1931-
  Victims and neighbors.

  Bibliography: p.
  Includes index.
  1. Jews—German (West)—Rhineland-Palatinate. 2. Holocaust,
Jewish (1939-1945)—Germany (West)—Rhineland-Palatinate. 3. Hol-
ocaust   survivors—Germany   (West)—Rhineland-Palatinate.   4.
Rhineland-Palatinate (Germany)—Ethnic relations. I. Title.
DS135.G4R485   1984   943'.43   83-25722

ISBN 0-89789-047-7
ISBN 0-89789-048-5 (pbk.)

Copyright © 1984 by Bergin & Garvey Publishers, Inc.

Published in 1984 by Bergin & Garvey Publishers, Inc.
670 Amherst Road
South Hadley, Massachusetts 01075

Printed in the United States of America

Contents

Foreword

More than one generation has passed since the twelve dark years of Nazi tyranny over Germany and Europe came to an end. Nevertheless, most of us, Jews certainly more intensely than others, still cannot fathom the causes that brought the long history of Jews in Germany to such a horrible end. Although a rather small minority in Germany—and to a high degree assimilated—Jews had made major contributions to German political, economic, and above all cultural life over a period of centuries. Notwithstanding the fact that full emancipation and equality of status was only attained through the foundation of the German empire, non-Jews and Germans of Jewish descent lived and cooperated with each other for decades—and in some places for centuries. As the author correctly states, "We were all the same kind of people."

To write about German Jews today means to write about the past and about a group of which many did not survive. And many of the survivors would never return. But even when Jews returned to Germany—those who were willing to forgive and who wanted to participate in building up a new democratic Germany side by side with those objectively responsible for genocide, mass murder, and "experimental" medicine—crimes unparalleled in world history—the few again who still lived in Germany, lived more or less in a secure niche, unwilling to attract attention. "It is for the dead and the living we must bear witness," says Elie Wiesel. And that is why we must ask uncomfortable questions, we cannot, we dare not treat history as entirely behind us. History accompanies us with every step we take. We the living, Jews and non-Jews, are victims and culprits alike.

Many, but not all Nazis rose up from the underworld. They were pushed forward, or better, they pushed themselves forward in a nation that had been proud of being at the hub of European civilization. To call Nazism the ideology of those who came from the losing side would be simplifying things too much. The Nazis could only be successful by gaining the active and passive support of large numbers of civil servants, of teachers and professors, of physicians who had taken the Hippocratic oath, of lawyers who had learned and memorized the tenets of justice, even of priests who had consecrated themselves to the service of God, and of millions of ordinary men and women.

Nazism was not rooted in abstract statutes. Nor did it confine its methods to anonymous and efficient gas chambers. It was created and borne by living persons. It was anchored not only in grand places of power and representation, but just as much in small towns and neighborhoods like Sonderburg, the hamlet both real and fictitious, in which the author sets her study. Sonderburg may be typical for the situation of Jewish citizens in pre-war Germany. What we do learn from this book is this: the reaction to Nazism was not programmed, neither was it implanted with genetic codes, nor could it be considered part of Germany's cultural heritage. The attitudes towards Nazism could range from active support to passive adjustment, from apathy in the face of Jews (and anti-Nazis from various origins, especially from the labor movement) being taunted and tortured to friendly helpfulness and passive or even heroic resistance.

Still, the question is this: what prevented, what hindered those who had gone to school with Jewish neighbors, who had worked with them in office, schools, factories and hospitals, who had spent leisure time with them in coffeehouses or at the "Stammtisch", what kept them from standing up for their friends and neighbors of Jewish faith?

Were they, were we all, so "ill equipped," as Frances Henry states? To answer by claiming "social barriers" is begging the question, since such barriers existed in the same degree elsewhere in Germany and in Europe. Anti-Semitism was both overt and covert in Sonderburg. The normal thing to do was to get along with one another, to live and let live. When does this principle turn into "minding one's own business"? At what point does laissez-faire turn into indifference, indifference into disrespect?

If history proves anything it is that too few people made conscious choices against evil. If there is any lesson to be learned from the extermination of millions of Jews, it is that decent men and women learn to make choices in favor of the good, and to do this before criminal power is established and gets stabilized. It is the one lesson history must teach, so that it does not repeat itself.

Willy Brandt
Bundestag
Bonn, West Germany

Preface

Much has been written about the Holocaust in recent years. In fact, there appears to be a resurgence of interest in the whole phenomenon of the Holocaust, perhaps spurred by the claims of those who say it never happened. Recently, there have been documentaries and films for the cinema and television, of which the popular *Sophie's Choice* is but one example. In addition, numerous testimonials and memoirs written by World War II survivors have been published. Historical studies written by scholars about this period also seem to be on the increase. If anything, this period of history had been underresearched, but now both scholarly and popular interest in the Holocaust, Hitlerism, and the experiences of survivors and their children, as well as other aspects of this period of history, has reached a new high.

This book is not about the Holocaust, but it does describe the situations and events that led up to it. It attempts to examine relationships between people—Jews and Gentiles—in one small town in Germany and in so doing may shed some light on why the persecution of the Jews took place.

Many people have contributed to the creation of this book. Obviously, it could not have been written without the splendid cooperation of the citizens of Sonderburg and the Jewish survivors from Sonderburg who now live in the United States. They were open and honest with me and allowed me to record their feelings and reminiscences. I am extremely indebted to John Miller and his family, who read an early draft of the manuscript and made important corrections and additions. Several members of my own family also read a draft and made suggestions for improvement. My mother died while this book was being written, but she was able to read an earlier version, and I am grateful for her encouragement, help, and support through all the stages of this project. I also owe a debt to colleagues and friends who read drafts and whose comments were particularly helpful. They include Rabbi Gunther Plaut, Gustav Thaiss, Ernest Lilienstein, and Evelyn Kallen. My thanks also go to Michael Kater, who encouraged me to adopt a broader historical framework and to look at Sonderburg in the context of the entire country. Raymond Wolff gave me access to some important archival material in his possession. Special thanks go to Sylvia Brown, who edited the manuscript in its early stages, and Kirsten Semple, who typed many drafts of it. I wish to thank my family and particularly my husband, who not only read chapters but critically encouraged me to do the project in the first place.

This book was made possible through a leave fellowship granted by the Social Science and Humanities Research Council of Canada. The research committee of the Faculty of Arts at York University was also generous in granting me several awards to carry out the project.

Interviews made in Sonderburg were recorded in German, and several quotes used in the book were recorded just as they were spoken in the dialect of Sonderburg. I translated the quotes into English. The translations are accurate and reflect the sentiment and spirit of the speakers. Quotes in German are not standard German, or *hochdeutsch*, but are in the particular dialect of the Sonderburg area.

As with the places in William S. Allen's *The Nazi Seizure of Power*, one will not find Sonderburg on the map of Germany. The place names and names of persons have been changed in order to protect the anonymity of the respondents. I do not think that these changes affect the narrative or the analysis of interethnic relations between Jews and non-Jews in Germany. The town here called "Sonderburg" is fairly typical of small towns in Germany and the experiences cited here would apply to many places.

To my father, who unfortunately died years before this project was started but whose spirit supported me throughout, and to my mother, whose determined efforts got us out of Germany and who even in the last months of her life contributed to the making of this book.

Home of author's grandparents in Sonderburg, 1918.

INTRODUCTION

My paternal grandparents lived in a little town called Sonderburg in the Rhineland area of Germany. My father, his sisters, and
brother grew up there, and I spent many holiday periods in Sonderburg when I was a very young child. The town then contained about
4,000 inhabitants and about 150 of them were Jewish. My grandparents had originally come from the village of Keltenburg, ten kilometers away. They owned a fairly large house on Wilhelmstrasse,
one of the main streets of the town. My grandfather had a small
retail shop downstairs and the family lived upstairs. The house was
surrounded by a courtyard, and in my mother's photo album there
is a picture of me at the age of three, stark naked, standing in a tin
bucket out in the courtyard, with my grandfather pouring water
over my head. In 1939, when I was seven years old, my parents were
finally able to migrate to the United States. Although my formative
years were spent in New York, where I grew up, I remember hearing
a great deal about Sonderburg. Friends and neighbors were often
mentioned with fondness by my parents. But curiously enough,
little was ever said about the growth of Nazism and its impact on

1

our lives. As a child, all I knew was that there was a war on and we were forced to leave Germany and come to the United States. I witnessed the hardships my parents endured by resettling in a new country and their remorse and guilt in not being able to effect the emigration of my grandparents, who were, along with several other elderly Jews, rounded up and deported to concentration camps in 1942. They were never heard of again. Sometimes bits and pieces of this story were told to me by my parents, uncle, and aunts, but perhaps because I was a young child and later an adolescent preoccupied with the usual teen-age concerns, the story was never told to me in any great detail. I was then not terribly interested in it either because I was struggling to overcome my German, albeit Jewish, identity in order to become, like my friends, 100 percent American. New Yorkers in the early forties did not differentiate between immigrant Jews and Gentiles, and for many I was German, maybe even a Nazi, in any case an enemy. It was to escape this stigma that I deliberately repressed any aspect of my Germanness, including the ability to speak the language, and I did not concern myself with the details of the German experience. In fact, I would tell people that I really came from Switzerland. Nevertheless, although I was only seven years old when we emigrated, I had memories of Germany and I never successfully repressed certain experiences.

I remember, for example, the invasion of our home by the SS—the elite military unit of the Nazi party that functioned as special police—during the infamous Kristallnacht. (Kristallnacht, or Crystal Night, so called because of the amount of glass that littered the streets on the morning of November 10, 1938, was the first major physical assault launched against Jewish homes and properties by the Nazi regime.) My parents and I lived in an apartment on the second floor of a two-story house in Kreuzen, a middle-sized city about one hour's drive from Frankfurt on the Main. My father, after finishing his residency in medicine in Kassel (where I was born), opened his medical practice in Kreuzen. Kreuzen is only fifty kilometers from Sonderburg, so that we were always in touch with our relatives. He had no sooner started his practice when, in 1935, Jewish physicians were pressured to close their offices. However, he had some faithful Gentile patients, who continued to use his medical services because they trusted his ability. Throughout the years 1935–38, he was thus able to eke out a modest income by practicing medicine unofficially. All that ended on November 9, 1938.

Wooden steps led up to our apartment and at about 2:00 A.M. heavy, pounding footsteps rushing up the stairs awakened us. In a moment, the glass doors leading to the apartment were smashed, and about five or six black-suited, heavily armed SS officers burst in and began smashing everything in sight. They were laughing, singing, and joking as they went about their business while we hovered in a corner of the living room. I remember most vividly their shiny, knee-high black leather boots, since at the age of six, I was just about knee-high to them. A very large wooden wardrobe stood against the bedroom wall and one of the men struck his ax through it and began throwing out its contents. Suddenly, I saw him grab my favorite doll, which was lying on the top shelf. I darted forward to retrieve the doll, only to be quickly pulled back by my mother as he laughingly wielded his ax to chop the doll in two. After destroying most of our goods and chucking several pieces of furniture through the windows, they departed. We felt lucky to be alive. The next morning two different officers, both of whom my father knew by name, came to the apartment and apologetically said that they had to take my father away. One of them, red-faced and embarrassed, said, "I hate to do this, Herr Doktor, you are the last one we are taking, but we must follow our orders." Later we learned that he had been sent to Dachau. Fearing that we too would be taken, my mother and I hid in a sympathetic neighbor's apartment and whenever we heard a noise, we quickly hid in a closet. During this time, my mother and I survived with the help of her old washerwoman, Frau Schmidt, who daily left a basket of food for us. This woman had worked for my parents for some years and could not allow Herr Doktor's wife to suffer, despite the fact that her two sons were SS officers and would surely have turned their mother in for aiding Jews.

My mother needed large sums of money to travel to different bureaucratic centers and especially to bribe various officials to secure my father's release from Dachau. Her Gentile brother-in-law gave her the sum of 10,000 marks, then a very substantial amount of money, which he delivered late one night after traveling well over 300 kilometers. He could not trust even his own bank to arrange such a transfer to my mother. Without this money, most of which was spent on bribes and later on securing passage out of Germany, my father would surely have died in Dachau. As a curious and ironic twist to this incident, in 1975 I visited my uncle, then old and dying of cancer in a hospital. I still did not know of his kindness to my family, and I made this visit rather reluctantly to a dying man whom

I did not even know. Upon my return to Canada, my mother was glad to learn what I had done because without his help we might all have died. I immediately wrote him a letter thanking him for his "old act of kindness," which he received the very day before he died.

Shortly after the war, my mother returned to visit her Gentile relatives. She also visited Kreuzen in order to find Frau Schmidt. After some searching, she located the old and very ill woman living in abject poverty in a single room. Both her sons had been killed during the war. She greeted my mother with tears but was happy to know that Frau Doktor was alive and well. Despite her resistance, my mother arranged for her to enter an old age home and paid the fees for the remainder of Frau Schmidt's life.

Other memories I have include my attending a special school for a few months. Jewish children by the mid-1930s were no longer allowed to attend the public schools. A friend and I, along with other Jewish children, had to meet in the basement of Herr Mannes's home about three blocks from my family's apartment. There Herr Mannes, a schoolteacher dismissed from his job, conducted a one-room school for Jewish children. Each row was a different grade and we small children sat in the first row, while the older children occupied the back rows. The youngest were taught counting with carefully collected empty egg shells. My most painful memory of this time was the way in which my friend and I were taunted by Nazi youths as we made our way back and forth to the small school. They would hurl insults, stones, and paper bags filled with manure at us while shouting "*Jud, Jud scheiss in die Tüt!*" (Jew, Jew, shit in the bag!).

As a result of my mother's many efforts, my father was eventually released from Dachau and sent back by train to Kreuzen. I remember his return; gaunt and weary, in his eagerness to embrace me he became entangled in a set of orange striped curtains that hung before my bed. A short time later, we left Germany by ship and arrived in New York in March 1939. I was then seven years old.

Throughout the rest of my childhood and adolescence in New York, I had a vague and somewhat intellectualized notion that we had been extremely lucky to have escaped the Holocaust. Life proceeded as I made my way through school and university, eventually entering graduate school to study anthropology. This discipline attracted me because of its dual nature, including both science and the humanities. I married twice and have had two children, one of whom, my young daughter, bears the same name as the doll chopped up many years earlier by the SS guards. Although I had many occasions earlier in my life to visit Germany, I never did so because I was never able to overcome the hostility and anger I felt toward the country and all things German. It was an animosity I carried with me for many years. Later, as I turned forty and entered midlife, the impact of my childhood in Germany and the experiences of my family and of millions of other Jews finally overwhelmed me to the point where I had to deal somehow with those years and experiences. At last I did what many people since the war have done; I returned to Germany to visit the places of my origin—where I was born, the town and the very apartment I had lived in, and Sonderburg, where I had spent so many holidays as a young child happily visiting my grandparents. That trip in 1975 was a profound and moving experience for me but it was not without its humorous aspects. I discovered, for example, that the hospital where I was born had been bombed during the war and in its place today stands a large, impressive, and obviously very successful Volkswagen dealership. When I entered it and spoke to a few people there, an old mechanic remembered the hospital and took me back to where their service department was and said, "Right here, on this spot, was the maternity ward."

I arrived in Sonderburg late on a Friday afternoon not knowing where to look for my grandparents' house. I was determined to do this pilgrimage on my own, without prior information as to addresses, names, and the like. I thought I would recognize the house, but, as it turned out, it had been modernized, and although I wandered up and down the streets in the old part of town, I could not find it. Ordinarily the police department would have had a record of any persons who had ever lived there, since in Germany all such details about residents are filed by the police. But it was the beginning of the weekend and the police station in this small town had already closed at midday. The town had also grown in size and its population had more than doubled in the intervening years. Feeling somewhat desperate at this point, I suddenly recalled my anthropological training and decided to look for some old people who might be able to tell me where my grandparents' house was located. As I walked down yet another street on this lovely late summer afternoon, I saw an old woman in conversation with an old man sitting shelling peas in the carport of their home. I walked in, introduced myself as Jacob Osterman's granddaughter and explained that I was looking for his house. The woman, startled, repeated the name wonderingly several times and told me that she knew the family well and that, of course, she knew where the house was. She immediately inquired after my father (Herr Doktor), my aunts, and other members of my family. Within minutes she turned to the period of the thirties and began telling me about the Jews, how much they had contributed to the town, how friendly everybody had always been, and what a terrible tragedy had befallen them. We spent many hours in conversation that day and the next. She brought in several of her neighbors who had also known the family. It became apparent to me that they were eager to talk about "those terrible times." Perhaps they welcomed the opportunity to talk because so many years had passed and because they were nearing the end of their lives. I also suspect that they had attempted to repress that whole period of their lives, with little success.

Upon my return to Canada, it occurred to me that this trip could be the groundwork for a splendid research project exploring and reconstructing the relationships between Jews and Gentiles in this small town. I felt that I might be the ideal researcher to carry out this project because of my personal ties to the town. Perhaps these old people would not be so willing to talk to a total stranger about that period in their lives. The project was carried out five years later, during my sabbatical year, and resulted in the present book.

The book is written from a dual perspective. On the one hand, it attempts to incorporate the tenets and methods of social anthropology or, perhaps more accurately, ethnohistory, in that it contains the usual material on the town's historic, social, and economic characteristics gathered from the census and other official documents as background to the dynamics of German Jewish and Gentile relationships.[1] The data have been gathered by the traditional techniques of anthropological fieldwork, using the intensive interview method with the town's elder Gentiles, most of whom are now in their seventies and eighties, and with a similar group of Jewish survivors now residing in the United States. Thirty-one people were interviewed in Germany and nineteen were tracked down in the United States. (Four or five Sonderburgers live in England or Israel, but they were not contacted for this study since they were all children during Hitler's times.) The snowball technique of gathering a sample was employed, one person giving me the names of others and so on. Although I carefully explained my professional role to my respondents, they received me and welcomed me not as a visiting scholar, but as the returned granddaughter of the Osterman family. When I explained my purpose, I was often greeted with "Yes, yes, you are going to write a book, but how is your father, what was your younger aunt's name, the one with all that curly hair?" My reaction to them was often equally emotional and personal, particularly when I was given the details of my own grandparents' deportation by eyewitnesses.

The book thus incorporates professional ethnohistory as well as subjective and personal family experiences.[2] Chapter 7 attempts to put Jewish and Gentile relationships into the theoretical perspective of ethnic relations research as conducted in social anthropology. The nonacademic reader may wish to skip that chapter. For the rest, I have attempted to maintain a descriptive, nontechnical style and tell the story as it was told to me by the survivors from both groups. These are the experiences of people who participated in this major historical event. I do not claim to portray the historical aspect of the period but rather how it was perceived by people. There may well be errors of historical fact in some of these accounts. Because of their enormous complexity, the regime's laws, which changed in their dealings with Jews between the early and the later thirties, were not always clearly understood by members of either group, especially in a small, somewhat isolated town such as Sonderburg. As Elie Wiesel notes in his Introduction to Sylvia Rothchild's *Voices from the Holocaust,* "in this book historical facts are less important than the manner in which the witness remembers and communicates them. The errors themselves—of memory or of perception—deserve a place in the dossier."[3] The same can be said of the present work.

Much has been written about the Nazi takeover of power in Germany.[4] The regime from the top has been thoroughly researched. There is also an increasing literature on the Holocaust in both the academic and the popular press.[5] To my knowledge, however, little if anything has been written about relationships in a small town. William S. Allen's work comes closest because it, too, focuses on one small town and employs the technique of social anthropology and ethnohistory to gather data, but his theme is the way in which the Nazis took power in one small community.[6]

However, a recent Ph.D. dissertation, written by E. Labsch-Benz at the University of Strasbourg and published in German, in some respects parallels this work. Labsch-Benz describes a similar set of accommodative patterns of interaction between Jews and Gentiles in Nonnenweier, but the emphasis in her work is on Jewish daily life and religious habits.[7] John K. Dickinson's *German and Jew: The Life and Death of Sigmund Stein* uses a detailed biographical approach to document the events in the life of Stein, who lived in a small community called Hochberg. There is some material about Jewish and Gentile relationships in Dickinson's work but its focus is on one man and his family.[8] Recently, a number of German scholars, in particular Martin Broszart, have been emphasizing the local and regional level in their sociological and political analysis of Bavaria.[9] Additionally, studies of the history of Jewish communities were undertaken in many of Germany's cities and towns. Most of these were written and published well after the war and their primary intention was to record historical facts surrounding Jewish life and death in Germany.[10]

By a curious coincidence, a project involving the "study" of Jews and Gentiles in a small town was released in 1981 as a film made for West German television. The film, *Now, After So Many Years*, examines the attitudes of Gentiles in the village of Rhina, who stoutly maintain that what happened to the Jews in their village was not the doing of the Rhina townfolk but the work of those from outside.[11] They insist on their innocence and some say that they either did not see the burning of the Jewish school and other acts of destruction or that they were not around at the time. Using the same technique as this book, the filmmakers, themselves German, interviewed on film a small number of Jewish survivors from Rhina now living in New York City. They all maintain that the townspeople themselves perpetrated the destruction and harassment and can even name those who participated. The film makes a dramatic political statement, indicting the Gentile Germans not only for their ideological, but also for their behavioral, complicity in the dictates of the Nazi regime as carried out against the Jews in their own village. It depicts the Germans as guilty, defensive liars and the Jews as helpless victims who claim, or at least one old lady claims, that they never received help from any of their neighbors. My own feeling is that it is the nature of the film medium to create, for the sake of a strong visual statement, views that are polar opposites. However, the events and peoples' reactions to them are too complex to be so neatly subsumed under the two opposing categories of villains and victims.

The present work is therefore something of a pioneer effort in that one of its main aims is to examine interethnic relations between German Jews and Gentiles living together in a small community during the 1920s and to document how these relationships changed during the 1930s with Hitler's rise to power. At the same time, however, the experiences of Jews in Sonderburg cannot be understood without reference to Jews elsewhere in Germany. Accordingly, the book includes references to broader occurrences taking place among German Jewry as a whole. The conclusion in Chapter 8, in fact, deliberately attempts to place the dynamics of interethnic processes in Sonderburg into the larger context of the Jewish experience in Germany. Thus, while this book should be read as a case study of one community, it became increasingly affected by the country's broader events. This, of course, raises the question of typicality. To what extent is Sonderburg representative of other small communities, not to mention the much larger urban Jewish population centers? The question is difficult to answer since there is little, if any, comparative research that focuses on interethnic relations in a small town as does the present work. However, an extrapolation from the growing literature on the history of Jewish communities throughout the country would indicate that patterns of interethnic relations before and after Hitler were in many respects similar. The pattern of Jewish occupational niching in the business and retailing sectors of the economy was common in the small towns throughout Germany. Geographic, regional, and demographic factors, as well as unique historical events, would probably explain whatever differences existed between small communities. On the whole, Sonderburg is fairly representative of towns of similar size in Germany.

But there were many important differences between urban and small-town Jewish life. The pattern of interethnic relationships also differed significantly. While these differences are beyond the scope of the present work, the interested reader might want to consult, for example, Sellenthin's history of the Jewish community in Berlin for an account of urban Jewish life.[12]

What emerges from an analysis of Sonderburg is a fairly typical picture of small-town life anywhere in the modern Western world. That is, there are certain patterned ways in which two groups structure their social interaction while maintaining their ethnic identity. Although Jews and their neighbors related at many levels and functioned as ordinary citizens of any small town, they nevertheless maintained their ethnic identity through the usual patterns of endogamous marriages, religious schooling for children, the establishment of a synagogue, maintaining of their own cemeteries, and the like. But, at the same time, they considered themselves and were considered by many Gentiles to be Germans. They were considerably integrated into the economic, social, cultural, and even political arenas, even though there was a substantial degree of economic niching—nearly half the Jews in Germany were in business and retailing. In the small community of Sonderburg and others like it, Jews and Gentiles before Hitler lived in friendly but carefully accommodative ways. The small Jewish community was relatively prosperous; the majority of the Jews were in business and retailing and a few were cattle traders. Thus, they were in an economic niche but nevertheless well integrated into the economy of the community. Some degree of mutual political participation and considerable social merging also linked the two communities (see Chapters 1 and 3). Culturally, Jews believed in and subscribed to the same values as did Gentiles. Jews in Sonderburg, like Jews elsewhere in Germany, were comfortable, even though they were never really totally assimilated into mainstream German society. Jews and Gentiles had accommodated themselves for generations to each other's presence, although, even in Sonderburg, Jews did face a degree of anti-Semitism prior to Hitler (see Chapters 3, 4, and 5). Anti-Semitism was, however, never really overt or serious enough to jeopardize these accommodative relationships until Hitler's accession to power.

Given this pattern between two ethnic groups with much in common, it is not surprising to discover that, as Nazi oppression of Jews began and accelerated throughout the thirties, both groups were ill equipped to handle the situation. German citizens in the main found it difficult to discriminate against and oppress people who had been their neighbors and often their employers for generations. Jews, on the other hand, found it equally difficult to believe in the seriousness of the regime's measures, particularly the measures to be implemented at the local community level. Slowly during the thirties, belief grew and more people began making efforts to migrate to other countries; finally, it was the infamous Kristallnacht of November 9, 1938, that indeed crystallized the truth for both groups. Given a long history of harmonious accommodative relationships between these two ethnic groups, it is not surprising that, as oppression from the top increased, local acts of kindness similarly increased. Perhaps one of the more interesting aspects of this book is that it documents the many acts of charity, kindness, and protectiveness shown toward Jewish citizens by their German neighbors (these are mainly described in Chapter 4). Indeed, had it not been for the help given certain individuals by their Gentile neighbors, at great risk to their own lives and security, many more people in this town would have perished in the Final Solution. These kind acts, as will be seen, are not major ones; they are the delivery of food parcels late at night, helping to mend furniture destroyed during

Kristallnacht, refusing to inform Nazi authorities of aid being given to Jewish families, and the like. They indicate that a measure of humanity was left in some of the ordinary population. Examining the ties in this one small town, and many others like it, we can assert that an entire population cannot be burdened with the sins of some.

Another objective of the present work is to undermine one of the major myths of the Third Reich, the myth of complicity. The horrors of the Holocaust and the war led to an indictment of an entire population and obscured the many ways in which some Gentiles tried to help Jews. The myth is best expressed in the commonly held opinion, particularly by surviving Jews, that "of course, they all knew what was happening" (about the camps and the Final Solution) or "everybody was guilty, they were all Nazis." Some Jews interviewed in this study gave this point of view while, at the same time, they applauded the efforts of those who helped them. A great deal of ambivalence has been expressed toward the German people and is reflected in the material gathered for this book. There were Germans whose behavior, even well into the thirties, indicated that they had not lost touch with humanity—a fact recently highlighted in a study of the French village of Le Chambon, where many ordinary villagers saved thousands of Jews from certain death.[13]

This is not to say that there were no Nazis in Sonderburg. Quite the contrary, as indicated in Chapter 2; there were many firmly committed members of the party and members of the SA and later the SS. It will also be noted in Chapter 4 that the sins of Kristallnacht were in the main committed by local people. But we need to establish a perspective capable of showing that, in the midst of practically the worst period in all of history, there were some people who were compassionate, kind, and loyal to their neighbors and were, in the words of an old German woman, *anständige Leute* (decent people).

In sum, then, this book has several objectives. First and foremost, it simply attempts to portray interethnic relations between Jews and Gentiles in one small community. Patterns of relationship are traced from the turn of the century to 1933, when Hitler came to power. This time period roughly corresponds to the ages of the respondents. The ways in which these interethnic patterns changed under Nazism during the thirties up to the outbreak of World War II are also traced and analyzed. There is no attempt to treat the later period of the Holocaust, except to describe what happened to the twelve Jews who had to remain in Sonderburg until their deportation in 1942. These changing patterns of interethnic relationships are mostly discussed in Chapters 3, 4, and 5. Chapter 1 examines the history of the community, focusing on the history of Jews. Chapter 2 emphasizes the Nazi power structure in Sonderburg and its effects on Jews, and their relations with Gentiles. Chapter 7 analyzes these patterns with reference to the theoretical literature on ethnicity and ethnic boundary mechanisms. What happened to the Jews of Sonderburg is discussed in Chapter 6, which describes their new lives in the United States and their feelings and reactions to their earlier experiences. The feelings and opinions of surviving Sonderburg Gentiles are also discussed in this chapter.

Interethnic relations even in one small town cannot be understood without reference to the process of assimilation. To what extent were Jews assimilated in Germany, particularly in Sonderburg? Can assimilation be defined against the background of anti-Semitism prevalent in Germany? The conclusions in Chapter 8 attempt to provide some answers to these questions.

Finally, a recurrent theme in the book, stressed in Chapter 5, is that some Germans in the country and in Sonderburg went out of their way to be helpful to Jews in their struggles to survive during the thirties and in their efforts to leave the country. Their helpfulness was invaluable in easing circumstances a little for the Jews. In Sonderburg, twelve old people were kept alive for several years because of the kindness of their neighbors. Obviously, not all Germans complied with the dictates of the regime.

Parents of a Jewish respondent coming in off the land, 1915.

1

THE HISTORY OF SONDERBURG: JEWS IN SONDERBURG

Sonderburg, situated in the middle part of the Rhine valley, is a very old town. Its name first appeared in church records in 1074, by which time some settlements had already been established. By the thirteenth century, it was under the jurisdiction of the archbishop of Mainz and was populated by several families of the lesser nobility, who purchased houses and property and were accordingly granted full municipal civil rights. During the Middle Ages the town, which was basically agricultural, was mainly inhabited by farmers, merchants, laborers, and a few families of the lower nobility. Although earliest population figures are not available, Sonderburg had about 800 inhabitants by the time of the Thirty Years' War in 1618.[1]

Throughout ensuing centuries and well into the twentieth century, the economy of the area had centered on agricultural pursuits such as farming, animal husbandry, fruit growing, viniculture, and, in the nineteenth century, tobacco growing. The land was originally distributed according to the principles of medieval feudalism. Several large estates belonged to the municipality, the Catholic church, and the noble families, whereas local farmers rented—or, rarely, owned—some small and medium-size farms. Markets played an important part in the economy since all produce not used for personal consumption or for payment to landlords was brought into the market in the town and offered for sale. A weekly market supplied direct food needs, whereas special annual markets were held to supply cattle, lumber, grain and other special needs. In addition to the markets, there were also merchants who dealt primarily in dry goods. Craftsmen, too, played an important role and enhanced the occupational diversity of the town. They included tanners, blacksmiths, carpenters, shoemakers, coach builders, and tailors. In large communities, groups of craftsmen formed guilds. In Sonderburg, which was small and primarily agricultural, only a few guilds for butchers and tanners were established. By 1772, however, there were 110 craftsmen of various kinds in the town. By and large, Sonderburg remained an agricultural area until the end of the nineteenth century. In 1832, a box factory and a printing establishment opened, followed in 1865 by a stocking factory, owned and operated by a Jewish family. Several other factories were opened around the turn of the century. By the early twentieth century, approximately 3,000 persons resided in Sonderburg. The economic life of Sonderburg, as elsewhere in Germany, was severely disrupted by World War I and the subsequent period of inflation. One of its main industries was forced to close and several of its banks were in severe difficulty. Despite these economic problems, the city grew and enlarged its boundaries during the 1920s. Sonderburg was also affected by unemployment created by the depression but its major industries were able to maintain themselves. The Jewish-owned hosiery mill, which produced a high-quality consumer product and had a considerable export trade, was only moderately affected. Since Sonderburg was in an agricultural area, produce and other foodstuffs were still readily available. In addition, at least 10–15 percent of the population were then still engaged in agriculture. By 1933, Sonderburg had a population of 4,357.

The Jews in Sonderburg

During the Middle Ages and afterward, Jews were allowed to live in the municipality and neighboring villages if they obtained special consent. In order to obtain a permit of settlement, Jews had to make a special payment and were afterward required to pay special taxes to municipal authorities. Jews were already living in Sonderburg in 1336, and in 1362 two Jewish merchants paid thirty guilders each in annual taxes. By 1418 there were at least four families, and by 1616 more Jews must have come into the community as it was by then large enough to support a Jewish school. These early Jews were primarily moneylenders, an occupation forbidden to Christians. They charged fairly high interest rates—which made them unpopular—such rates being necessary to protect their investments. They also traded in cattle, wine, and dry goods. Between 1348 and 1350 various oppressive measures were taken against Jews on the pretext that God's wrath at their part in killing Christ required appeasement. In reality, religious controversies, as well as the unpopularity of Jewish moneylenders, were the reasons for discrimination. Besides, noblemen and commoners alike wanted to rid themselves of inconvenient creditors. At various other times in its history, the Jewish community was either ostracized or banished when local people owed them too much money. Christian merchants were in competition with Jewish merchants and frequent altercations took place, often leading to demands that the Jews be turned out, thus eliminating disadvantageous competition. The early history of the Jews in Sonderburg (or Germany) indicates that they were never fully accepted into contemporary, mainstream society and that they led a precarious existence.

In a special census of Sonderburg residents undertaken in 1743, four Jewish household heads were listed out of several hundred. One of these Jewish families, with surname slightly modernized in spelling, existed in the town until the early 1930s, when the family emigrated to the United States. Most Sonderburg Jews in modern times could trace their ancestry back to the seventeenth or eighteenth century and most of them originated in the smaller villages around Sonderburg.

Little is known of the community in terms of existing published sources. But a civic document from the beginning of the nineteenth century notes that a Jewish managing committee was elected from among the male members of the community to serve for a period of three years. This and subsequent elections until 1888 were supervised by the mayor of the town and confirmed by the Hebrew community in Bonn. The election of these committees confirms that Jews were forming a private religious community managed by an elected committee of adult men. Worship costs and other costs were collected by the civic tax authorities. At this time, Jews were subject to the Prussian laws of 1847, guaranteeing them freedom to live where they pleased; changes in residence no longer needed official approval. Although Jews were still excluded from leading positions, they could nevertheless be appointed members of the town council committees or civic deputies. Several men of the more prominent Jewish families served the town in these capacities from 1885 onward. Jews could also freely purchase property and vote in all elections.

Until 1926, the Jews in Sonderburg, together with those of the neighboring villages, belonged to the Gemeinde, or corporation of one of the nearby cities. The Gemeinde was a public body and all Jews were registered into it at birth. Jews were taxed by the state as members of the Gemeinde in order to maintain their religious institutions, such as synagogues and cemeteries, to provide religious education, and to disburse charity to the poor.

That the community was still fairly small is evidenced by the fact that the establishment of a Gemeinde to permit tax collection was repeatedly rejected by the Jews in Sonderburg. In 1866 local Jews attempted to establish a corporation with their fellow Jews in two neighboring towns; this was rejected by the latter groups, which did not want to travel to Sonderburg. The formation of a Jewish community as a corporate body of the public law within Sonderburg came about only in 1924–26, when a committee proposed the motion and elected nine representatives and three members to form a managing committee. After the necessary administrative and statutory procedures, the motion came into effect in April 1926, only seven years before the Third Reich was elected to office and began its oppression of Jewish communities everywhere in Germany. Such delay in forming the corporation also suggests that in the early twenties Jews had enormous confidence in their security and their positions in the community. They had no fears for their future.

With respect to its history and development, Sonderburg was like most small towns with a minority Jewish population. While the vast majority of the Jews in Germany lived in cities, the importance of the smaller town and village Jew cannot be underestimated since most of the urban dwellers had rural roots and migrated to the cities from the middle of the nineteenth century onward. These urban migrations were largely in response to the greater freedom that Jews were entitled to under the provisions of the so-called Prussian Laws of 1847. They were allowed to move freely about the country and many began leaving towns and villages in search of

greater employment and financial opportunities in cities. W.J. Cahnman estimates that a hundred years before Nazism, about 90 percent
of Jews were living in villages and small country towns.[2] As in
Sonderburg, the majority of rural Jews were engaged in cattle trading
and some owned land. Later, rural Jews began to open retail shops
selling dry goods and notions of the kind formerly sold by their
itinerant peddler forefathers. In other small towns, as in Sonderburg,
garment manufacturers, cotton, hide, and leather wholesalers, as
well as professional occupations, began to diversify the employment
pattern of rural Jews. Cahnman notes that "village Jews were not
peasants of a different ethnicity. They were urbanites transmuted
into rural folk."[3] In the Middle Ages urban Jews were expelled from
the city centers and sought refuge in villages. In the nineteenth
century the process began to reverse as the movement back to urban
areas took place, leaving smaller Jewish communities in the villages
and small towns. Cahnman describes the nineteenth-century rural
Jews as follows:

> Miserable as the country Jews may have been in the eighteenth
> century, they became the leaders in modernity in the places they
> resided in the nineteenth century. They awakened new needs and
> desires, promoted voluntary associations and cultural activities
> . . . [they] frequently took the initiative in suggesting better means
> of communication and advanced schools, they supported social
> institutions such as orphan asylums and hospitals, their houses
> were larger and more solidly built, their furniture more represent-
> ative of the newest taste, their meals more opulent, and their wives
> and daughters better groomed and dressed after the newest fashion.[4]

This description accurately fits the activities and style of life as
lived by Jews in Sonderburg.

Although a corporate community, or Gemeinde, did not come
into being until the twentieth century, the Jews in Sonderburg did
build a synagogue, which was opened in 1858. Before then, the
services were held in a private home that could only accommodate
two dozen people, which became increasingly inconvenient. A small
site was purchased by a Mr. Spath, then a prominent member of the
community. Two-thirds of the construction costs were raised by the
Jewish community through the collection of a special synagogue
tax. One-sixth came from legacies and donations and the remaining
one-sixth was contributed by the town in the form of a subsidy. An
adjacent site, also belonging to the community, housed the religious
teacher. These sites served the religious needs of the Jews until

1938, when the synagogue was partially destroyed during Kristall-nacht. The site was later restored and in 1951 it came into the possession of the city, which leased it to a department store owner. Today it is being used as a furniture warehouse.

The Jewish cemetery, situated on one of the hills overlooking the town, had been a private burial ground for one Jewish family; shortly after 1860, the property rights for the cemetery were given to the community in the form of a legacy and from then on used to bury all Jewish dead. In 1930 two prominent Jews, by their own wish and the town council's agreement, were buried in the munic-ipal cemetery. In 1933, however, both were transferred to the Jewish cemetery by order of the Nazi regime. The cemetery, along with other Jewish properties, was destroyed during Kristallnacht, and most of the headstones were defaced and toppled with axes. It was reconstructed shortly after the war as part of the postwar restoration of Jewish property. It has been maintained ever since by the Jewish community in nearby Kreuzen with the help of municipal funds.

In addition to building the synagogue, maintaining the ceme-tery, and granting corporate status to the community, the group also employed a full-time religious leader—a cantor—who officiated at services, births, deaths, and marriages. He was also in charge of the religious instruction of the children. From the age of six till they turned fifteen, Jewish children attended religious school on Sundays. Ordinary schooling, of course, took place in the public schools, which both Jews and Gentiles attended. Thus, for almost one hundred years, from approximately the middle of the nineteenth century, the Jewish community in Sonderburg, although always fairly small, was assured of its own religious and educational facil-ities.

From the turn of the century to 1933, there were approximately 150 Jews living in Sonderburg. They were divided into thirty-four families. Most of these families had lived in the area for generations and sixty-five persons were born in the town. Most of the remainder came from the nearby villages—Mettheim, Stattheim, Steinhardt, and others. Four persons came from cities further away and all four were women who had married men from Sonderburg and resettled there. Jews thus constituted less than 4 percent (3.4 percent) of the population.[5] It was a fairly old and settled community, and a con-siderable amount of intermarriage between the families had taken place so that many of the 150 residents were related to each other at some level. Marriage patterns followed the rules of endogamy, and for the most part intermarriages between Jews and Christians here were rare. Despite their relatively small numbers, Jews were, by virture of their occupations, prominent citizens in the town and their influence in the local economy was out of proportion to their numbers.

As in other small towns and villages in Germany that contained small Jewish communities, trade and commerce were their predominant occupations. The most influential family in the town was undoubtedly the Millers, owners of a large hosiery mill and factory. In 1865, Mrs. Sara Miller was left widowed with nine children. She began knitting stockings in her home in order to support herself and the children. Soon she bought and installed a manual knitting machine and the production of stockings en masse began. A factory and mill were constructed in 1875, and the business kept expanding until it became the largest firm in the area, employing, at its height, as many as 800 workers. In addition, piecework done at home by women in Sonderburg and neighboring villages brought part-time employment and wages to many more families. The firm was managed by successive generations of Millers until 1938, when the director was finally forced to emigrate to the United States. The family reacquired ownership in 1948 and ran the business until 1972, when it was sold to a large corporation. Part of the original enterprise is still being run by the corporation as a carpet factory. The Millers were the richest family in the area, and they and two Gentile families, who also owned factories, were the largest employers in Sonderburg and its environs. Their prominence did not prevent their persecution by the Nazis, however, since the whole family was forced to flee, except for its patriarch, the son of the founder, who was deported to a concentration camp in 1942.

Although the Jewish community enjoyed its own religious facilities, it was not exceptionally religious. According to my respondents, there were no really Orthodox families in Sonderburg and most seemed to subscribe to some form of liberal Judaism. This was in keeping with German Jewry elsewhere in the country. By the start of the twentieth century, only 10–15 percent of the population was Orthodox. Since many Jews wished to assimilate into mainstream society, Orthodox practices fell by the wayside. Despite, or perhaps because of, the presence of considerable anti-Semitism in the nineteenth and early twentieth centuries, most Jews and Gentiles felt that a retreat from orthodoxy might reduce discrimination. Thus the Jewish community transformed the tenets of the older medieval Orthodox concepts of Jewry. A form of liberal Judaism came into being in the nineteenth century because of the desire to eliminate more obvious differences and, short of actual conversion, to become as much like Christians as possible. I. Shorsch notes that for true emancipation, most sectors of the political spectrum agreed that conversion to Christianity would be necessary. "Reform spokesmen . . . lowered the price to a religious accommodation that would diminish and conceal Jewish religious distinctiveness . . . they labored to prepare Judaism for integration." Jewish religious leaders "overhauled traditional Judaism, especially its theology and juridical claims, to a far greater extent than they were willing to admit." Despite the "reform movement which made the greatest investment to allay the prejudices and earn the good will of Germans opposed to or ambivalent about emancipation," most Germans continued to feel that total conversion was the only answer, while a "strident minority" in the nineteenth century felt that even conversion would not eradicate the racial and religious marks of Judaism.[6]

A form of liberal Judaism, somewhat similar to Conservative Judaism as practiced in the United States, developed in Germany as a result of the attempt by Jewish leaders to integrate the Jewish population more fully into the dominant society. Most of the Jews in Sonderburg adhered to this form of Judaism. They attended synagogue on the High Holidays, on Friday evenings, and on the Sabbath. Synagogue services were completely in Hebrew, but certain sermons were delivered in German. Men sat toward the front and women sat in the back. Children were sent to religious school and the boys were bar mitzvahed. Ceremonial occasions such as births, weddings, and deaths were kept according to Jewish rites. Dietary laws, traditions with respect to dress, ritual cleanliness of women and other laws associated with Orthodox forms of Judaism were not observed. Identifying with Jewish heritage and aspects of Jewish culture and belonging to the Jewish community were more important than Orthodox religious observances for the Jews in Sonderburg and, in fact, the remainder of the country.

Zionism had little active support among the Sonderburg Jews although some were quite sympathetic to it. In the 1920s and 1930s only a few people emigrated to Palestine—one of them a physician who, with his family, became Zionist in the late twenties. Another young woman joined a Zionist youth group while studying in Cologne and emigrated in 1932. Here, as elsewhere in Germany, Zionism had little direct influence in the Jewish community, whose primary aim was integration into German society. Most Jews were therefore not attracted to the ideal of creating a separate Jewish state, although the ideology of Zionism struck a responsive chord in some Jews. The Zionist Federation of Germany had only some 10,000 members in 1933 as compared to the Zentralverein (The Central Association of German Citizens of Jewish Faith), or ZV, "whose membership in 1933 of 70,000 probably comprised 60 percent of all Jewish families."[7] The Zionists were, nevertheless, a strong minority amongst the Jews in Germany. As Lucy S. Dawidowicz points out, "The Zionists and the *Ostjuden* (East European Jews)—to some extent congruent—were the more conspicuous minorities among German Jews, for they challenged the central tenet of German-Jewish existence—Jewish belongingness to Germany."[8] Originally, Zionism was spearheaded by intellectuals and academicians. Later, migrant East European Jews joined the movement, which further increased the chasm between them and native German Jews. By and large, Zionists in Germany were either East European Jews or intellectuals attracted to the idea of a Jewish state. The former group, feeling uncomfortable in Germany and alienated from native German Jewry, derived comfort from the idea of creating a homeland. The Jews in Sonderburg were "native," or German, Jews and no one of East European origin ever settled there. Thus, the Zionist movement had little direct impact on the Jewish community in Sonderburg.

Jewish Commercial Life in Sonderburg: The Miller Stocking Factory

As noted earlier, the Miller stocking factory and mill was the largest employer in the area and as such it was kept open until the end of 1938. The story of how the firm did business during the Nazi era is not only interesting, but also fairly typical of large-scale Jewish enterprises during this period.

In 1932 the director, Albert Miller, took on his son-in-law, Dr. Ritter, to run the firm, which he was to do until 1938. In the beginning, the family as a whole did not believe that the Nazi takeover would last; on the other hand, some of the younger members were disillusioned and three of them left Germany for the United States in 1935. Mr. Miller, urged by his family, began making efforts to sell the firm in 1936, when he received a rather good offer for it. He took a holiday in Switzerland and thought it over but upon his return canceled the transaction. His son John recalled that even earlier, while on a trip to Italy in 1934, the family chauffeur advised his father to sell the business: "It was early in 1934; my mother and

I were sitting in the back seat and the chauffeur said, 'Mr. Miller, get out of here, sell your things, get out of Germany.' Another man, a sort of body guard, also in the car (who turned vicious later and became a Nazi), also advised my father, 'sell everything, leave.' The firm was eventually sold to these same people at a much lower price than was previously negotiated. But my parents reneged on emigrating because they felt they could live it through, they could survive." Mr. Miller's earlier decision to renege on the sale transaction was apparently based on several reasons. First, he still believed that the Nazi regime would end and things would return to normal for the Jews. Second, the firm had kept all its customers, both in the internal German market and abroad, where the Millers traded extensively. Since it had many foreign customers, the firm earned much-needed foreign exchange for the regime. The regime in fact did not oppose the large Jewish firms in Germany either because they were foreign exchange earners or because in some cases no other firms had the managerial skills to take over Jewish businesses. By 1937, however, the firm was allowed to purchase only 60 percent of its usual raw materials, wool and cotton, but at the same time it was ordered not to dismiss any workers. Thus, in 1937 and early 1938, its production fell off but the overhead in labor costs remained. This last edict finally convinced the owner to sell. By then, however, the offer for the firm from the same company was only about a third of what it had been in 1936. The Millers thus were forced to sell for practically nothing.

Dr. Ritter, the son-in-law and active director of the firm during the thirties, describes how business was carried out under the regime: "It did not take too long to see that we as Jews could not survive in the Nazi society. Most of our German friends were afraid to associate with us. Some were even afraid to come and see us under cover of darkness. They could lose their jobs and possessions. Everything was organized after the 'führer' principle. As Hitler was Führer of the Third Reich, so we had a führer of our labor force and every firm and corporation had to have a führer to represent the firm or organization. I had the dubious honor of becoming führer of our firm."

Apparently, this involved mediating between the regime and the workers and representing the firm at official meetings. Dr. Ritter, as führer, was also required to give addresses to the workers on their duty to keep up productivity for the Reich. It is indeed ironic to consider that a Jew was the official representative or middleman between a Gentile work force and the Nazi regime. Dr. Ritter also recounts the help he received in running the firm from some of his workers. In one specific instance,

> One of our longtime employees came and told me that he would
> join the party, not out of conviction, but to keep me informed of
> what was going on in the local Nazi party, and he kept his word
> to the last. In 1933, there were general elections but you could
> only vote yes or no for the Nazi candidate. We always went to
> Luxembourg to escape the vote. One Monday morning after the
> election, it was announced that Sonderburg had voted 100 percent
> for the Nazis. But my friend told me that some of our workers had
> voted against Hitler and the local head of the party had reported
> a 100 percent vote to his superior. The local head knew the names
> of the workers who were against the party and came to force me
> to dismiss them, which would mean that they would become un-
> employable. My friend advised me to be firm against any dismissal
> because the local Nazi was afraid to push too hard, otherwise his
> higher-ups would hear that he had failed in his job.

This was one example where the local Nazis attempted to put pressure on the firm but their attempt was unsuccessful. As Dr. Ritter
explains,

> In the afternoon, the local Nazi leader appeared in my office with
> two of his henchmen. Before sitting down, he took his revolver out
> of its holster and put it on the table. Then he took out a list of
> about ten people employed in the mill. He said he wanted the
> dismissal of all ten immediately. But with my secret information,
> I was in the driver's seat and asked him why should I dismiss my
> people without a reason. To my demand for a reason he merely
> said it was a party matter. I said it was my responsibility as führer
> to contact his superiors but this he wouldn't let me do, so after
> more talk, he packed his revolver and with his two gangsters
> disappeared. In leaving he said to me, "Too bad you are a Jew, we
> could use you."

In this case, a loyal employee actively helped to keep the firm intact;
but not all employees were that loyal to the Jewish management.
A number of workers joined the party early and were active and
committed Nazis while they continued to earn their livelihood from
Jewish employers. Dr. Ritter describes another situation where he,
as a Nazi representative, was put into a conflicting situation.

> Another close situation was the party rally, which was held in the
> mill. Some of the Nazi big shots from out of town had come and
> I as the führer had to sit with them on the stage facing the crowd.

Representing our workers was one of the lowest of the low. During the meeting he accused me of sabotaging the ideas and will of the Führer. I really got scared and at the same time furious. I had kept a diary of all the things he had done wrong. After he was through, I got up and told the assembled crowd what kind of guy he was, that he was drunk a lot, and smoked under the rafters endangering the lives of his fellow workers. At the end I got applause. Next day he was dismissed.

The loyal employee also warned management whenever an internal revenue check was imminent. One of the techniques of harassment used by the Nazis was frequent tax checks in order to make sure that the family was not, under cover of the firm, spiriting out private monies for their own use. Thus, the internal revenue people came every few months, and Dr. Ritter recalls, "I was so nervous from it, that every morning I threw up." The firm was very careful, however, to keep its books in order, never giving the Nazis any reason to crack down on them. In the last year of the firm's operation, when the remaining family became desperate to leave Germany, they converted the corporation into a partnership so that both directors could convert their stock into capital. Then the final attempt at harassment came: "Our capital could not be taken out immediately as the law required a six-month waiting period. At the same time, we were again audited. New prices were established for us—every item we produced needed to be priced. We were found guilty by the price control board for allegedly making a pricing mistake and were fined 2,000 marks." This was clearly a strategy whereby a large sum of money could be extracted from the firm and donated to the Riech's coffers before the company was actually sold to an Aryan owner.

What is especially interesting about these incidents and the story of the mill's operation under Nazism is that, despite a few attempts at harassment, management was usually left alone to conduct business. Although the owners were unable to withdraw their own profits (since their personal bankbooks had been confiscated), they could on occasion, by saving vacation money while abroad, smuggle some funds into the United States. Aside from this restriction, business under the Nazis went on as usual. Apparently, other large Jewish-owned companies receives similar treatment. As long as they were earning tax revenue and the highly prized foreign exchange for the government, they were, on the whole, left alone. This was, of course, not the case for the small retail shopkeepers and other smaller businesses, which were forced to close by 1935. The rich Jews were unmolested and, as Dr. Ritter repeatedly notes, "our customers and most of our employees stayed with us. We could still visit our customers any time and some of our most valuable workers, the bookkeeper and the accountant, for example, were not afraid to visit us and enter through the front door!" Dr. Ritter was still visiting customers and taking orders until a few weeks before his departure for the United States. He recalls taking a business trip to Holland; on the train, Nazi officers removed his passport, but it was eventually returned.

The story of the Miller firm is, however, an isolated case as far as Sonderburg was concerned. The second largest Jewish-owned business, a moderate-sized department store, came under severe pressure in the mid-thirties; its owners finally leased it in 1935. Kahn's department store was started by Isaac Kahn in 1878 as a small dry goods establishment. The French occupation of the area after World War I resulted in large numbers of troops and officers being quartered in Sonderburg; some older buildings were renovated into apartments to serve as their living quarters. Furnishing and appliances for the apartments could not then be supplied by existing Sonderburg stores, so Richard Kahn, Isaac's son, consented to purchase and deliver the required furniture and appliances from larger neighboring cities. A short time later, Richard, sensing the needs of the community as a result of this experience, permanently expanded his father's business to include furniture, appliances, and clothing. In 1929, an entirely new store was built, owned and operated by Richard and his brother-in-law. The store employed some fifty sales and administrative personnel, about two-thirds of them Gentiles. The firm thrived until the early thirties, when business declined. In 1934, Oskar Schmidt became an employee in the firm. During this time, Nazi hooligans repeatedly defaced the property and harassed its owner. The following year the business was rented to a merchant in a nearby town but, after the war, Schmidt purchased the firm when Kahn and his brother-in-law returned to settle their affairs. The department store today carries the Schmidt name and is still a thriving commercial enterprise.

In addition to these large Jewish-owned businesses, there were seven more retail dry goods and clothing stores, one shoe store, two groceries (one also sold secondhand goods and the other dealt in coal and fodder, as well as foodstuffs), one cattle dealer, two butcher shops and one innkeeper—all owned and operated by Jewish families. Three families ran a livery and horse-trading business, which primarily involved buying horses from farmers for resale in the town and neighboring cities. Thus a total of nineteen independent commercial businesses, ranging from a large industrial complex to a very small family-run dry goods shop, were owned and managed by Jewish families in Sonderburg before 1933. While there were at least two Christian-owned industries and several non-Jewish shops and cafes in the town, most of the retail trade was conducted by Jews. These trades kept the entire Jewish population at work and in relatively comfortable middle-class circumstances. Underrepresented in this small town were the professions, the clothing trades, non-retail commercial enterprises, and the civil service.

In terms of comparison with the rest of the population of Sonderburg, the occupational breakdown of the town in the census of 1933 indicates that the majority of employed inhabitants—2,189— were in industrial and manual labor jobs, 720 persons were in trade and commerce, and 426 were employed on the land or in forestry. Approximately 10 percent of the labor force was still engaged in farming and, of course, the majority owned their own land. The lands were dispersed throughout the areas surrounding the town. Farmers would work their land but live in Sonderburg, traveling to and fro daily. It was not unusual to own a piece of land in one place, and another three kilometers away. This pattern of land usage developed as a result of traditional inheritance patterns, which followed the laws of primogeniture; as far as can be ascertained by respondents, none of the Jews in Sonderburg was a landowner. In addition, there were 771 civil servants and 651 self-employed persons.[9] These figures show that Sonderburg was basically a working-class community in terms of occupation and income, with a small middle class and a very small upper class—comprising three or four families, one of which was Jewish. Evangelical Protestantism was the dominant religion—64 percent of the population was Protestant, 32.37 percent Catholic and 3.4 percent Jewish. The Jews by and large were overrepresented in the business sector and completely unrepresented in the civil service. Their occupational standing made them essentially middle class, although there were at least two very poor families in the Jewish community. In fact, several of the Gentile respondents interviewed in Sonderburg referred to the Jews as being "bessere Leute, geschäfts Leute" (better people, shopkeepers). Thus in a predominantly working-class town, where the small Gentile middle class was composed mainly of officials, civil servants, and a few professionals, Jews, despite their small number, were very prominent in this class.

Class status is here defined primarily by the occupational and income status of the family.[10] Thus the size of the Millers' operation would automatically place them in the upper class, whereas the ownership of a retail shop, regardless of its size, conferred middle-class status on its proprietors as far as the Gentile population was concerned. Within the Jewish community, however, class status was distinguished according to the size and income-earning potential of the business. Additionally, owning a retail haberdashery conferred higher status than did owning a butcher shop. Both Jews and Gentiles considered horse and cattle traders to be of lower status than retailers, although one family involved in the horse-trading business earned far more income than did the majority of small retailers. The Jews also recognized other dimensions of status, such as social and educational achievement. One family, for example, ran a succession of small businesses but through financial mismanagement had to declare bankruptcy twice. Their status was solidly middle class among both Jews and Gentiles because the head of the household was educated and could speak, read, and write in *hochdeutsch* (High German); he was also known to be widely read in literature, philosophy, and the arts. Another family owned a small haberdashery that barely supported it, but its head was known as a poet, a man of literature, and *sehr gebildet* (very cultured). Accordingly, their status in both groups was higher than their economic circumstances dictated. Despite these internal class differentiations, the majority of the Jews were considered by themselves and by Gentiles to be middle class.

This class pattern is in keeping with the Jewish community in Germany as a whole. Nearly two-thirds of the 500,000 Jews in the country were engaged in trade and commerce, one-quarter worked in industry and manual trades, and about one-eighth were in the public service and the professions, mainly law and medicine. Many urban Jews were represented in the professions and the civil service, whereas in the smaller communities the majority of Jews were in trade and commerce. Their overall socioeconomic position in this century, particularly during the period of the Weimar Republic following World War I, was overwhelmingly middle class. This "position reflected the historical circumstances of the Jewish situation in a Christian society and the opportunities offered by a rapidly expanding industrialized Germany of the late 19th century."[11] The Jewish community's comparative wealth was a factor in the hostility directed at it by a substantial portion of the German population. The enforced closure of its businesses during the mid-1930s provided considerable relief for Gentile debtors. Some of the storm troopers who vandalized and destroyed Jewish homes and properties during the Kristallnacht of November 9 and 10, 1938, were those who still owed money to Jewish merchants and were only too happy to clear their debts in this manner. Mr. Kahn, when he leased his firm in 1935, was allegedly left with thousands of marks in unpaid bills; this was also true of the smaller merchants, though the unpaid amounts were, of course, smaller.

The Jewish community in Sonderburg, though it numbered only 150 individuals, was nevertheless an established, old, and prosperous community, with an economic and social influence far more widespread than its small number might suggest. Although the community had completely disappeared by 1942, the Jewish presence was again felt in 1950, when several commemorative events took place in the town. These will be described in Chapter 5. During the early thirties, Sonderburg, like the rest of Germany, was overwhelmingly affected by the forces of Nazism. No overview of the community can be complete without an examination of Nazism in Sonderburg.

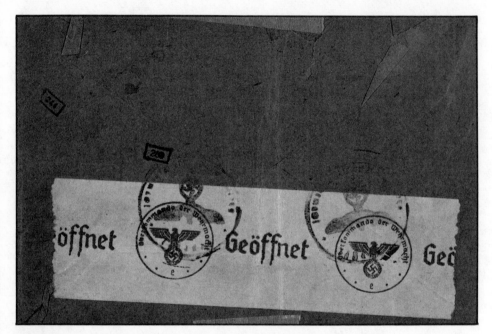

Example of a censored letter from 1940 which arrived marked "opened" and stamped with "by high command of the army".

2

THE NAZI POWER STRUCTURE
IN SONDERBURG

The organizational structure of Nazism and of the National Socialist State was extremely complex, and a detailed examination of it is beyond the scope of this book.[1] The main concern of this chapter is to describe those organizational and ideological facets of Nazism that affected the small community of Sonderburg.

During the early 1930s, Sonderburg had a population of almost 4,000 residents. Of these, approximately 600 were card-carrying members of the Nazi party, including about 100 hard-core or very committed party members, who were also members of the SA and later the SS.[2] (I will refer to the National Socialist German Workers' Party—the Nazis—as 'the party' throughout this book.) The SA, or Sturmabteilungen (Storm Troops), was the major paramilitary arm of the National Socialist State; by the end of 1933, it claimed four million members. Hitler began to regard the SA as a threat to his authority and ordered a purge. By 1934, the authority of the SA was undermined and the SS, or Schutzstaffel (Defense Corps), which had been part of the SA, increased its momentum. The SS had originally been created as an armed formation within the SA to protect Hitler and other top party leaders. When Himmler was appointed its director, he reinforced its elitist image and essentially converted it into an elite brotherhood selected according to racial criteria. As Dawidowicz notes, it was "permeated with a racial mystique imbued with medieval chivalric concepts of loyalty, honor, bravery and the like." The SS men were distinguished from SA members by their black uniform; the SA men wore brown shirts. The SS had as its task "primarily to carry out policy duties within the party," and on induction a recruit had to swear an oath of personal allegiance to Hitler.[3] Under Himmler's leadership, the SS grew rapidly until, by the eve of the war, it had nearly a quarter of a million members. The SS also undertook spying, surveillance, and intelligence functions in the towns and cities of the country. Thus, it did some of the same jobs as the official Secret State Police, more familiarly known as the Gestapo. Both the SS and the Gestapo came under Himmler's command and the two units were eventually merged.

In Sonderburg there were about seventy members of the SA and approximately thirty members of the SS during the 1930s. These figures are estimates made by Jewish and Gentile respondents, and they are roughly comparable to those for the small town of Thalberg described by William S. Allen. He notes, for example, that "there were not more than fifty members of the SA before 1933, though it seemed to most townspeople that there were anywhere from three to eight times as many."[4] In Thalberg, as in Sonderburg and elsewhere, SA men from surrounding areas would be called in to impress the populace at public functions.

The SA attracted the young and unemployed, called by many Sonderburgers the "Lumpen," or hooligans. They were rough, uneducated and primarily of working-class origin. The early SA contingent in Sonderburg, as elsewhere, attracted "the no goods, the down and outers who never amounted to anything, those who never could hold down a job," as several respondents described them. They were, nevertheless, increasingly disciplined and formed a brutal and terroristic group that threatened the Germans, as well as, of course, the Jews, their primary targets. Frau Tiller, one of the Gentile respondents, remembered that "I was always afraid of them, they would attack anybody. They were never the kind of people we associated with, they were *unanständig* [indecent]." The SS with its elitist image attracted more middle-class and professional people.

Prominent SS members in Sonderburg included several schoolteachers, the town's leading veterinarian, several highly placed civil servants, a doctor, and a leading judge.

Although there were only a hundred or so committed Nazis, they were, in the words of one Jewish respondent, "real terrors." She recalled that "it was not just the hundred in Sonderburg; they came from the smaller towns like Stattheim and Steinhart and they grew and grew and when they passed our house and sang 'Wenn vom Messer spritzt das Juden Blut, dann geht's noch mal so gut' (when Jewish blood flows from the knife, then everything goes well—a famous SA marching song) and I slept in the front room, I couldn't sleep, it was terrible."

Each town or community had a local Nazi chapter led by a town leader, or führer, called an *Ortsgruppenleiter*. In this town Fritz Dansk, a very early supporter of Hitler and a former member of the SA, occupied the position. Dansk was a younger son of a large and influential family that owned and managed the town's leading health resort. The family owned a large tract of land across the River, where, for many years, people came from distant places in order to rest and recuperate. Several of the Dansk family joined the cause early on and Fritz was one of the first. He was known as a ne'er-do-well who had attempted several careers but failed in each. When the Nazis came to power, he was operating a shoe store bought for him by the family but had little success with it and had been forced to declare bankruptcy. Joining the Nazis was for him the answer to a life of business and career failure. Being one of the first members in Sonderburg and possessing a dominant, charismatic personality, Dansk quickly rose in the infant hierarchy and become town führer. Under him were grouped several assistants or aides and then the rank and file members. As town fürher, he received his orders from a wider area superintendent but the day-to-day functions of Nazism in Sonderburg were left to Dansk and his assistants.

Most of this work involved the harassment of Jews through insults, name-calling, closing their businesses, and the like. He also organized rallies, marches, and demonstrations; on the infamous Kristallnacht, he sorted the members into small groups and sent them on their assignments. Apparently, Sonderburg did not have a large enough contingent to carry out the Kristallnacht raids, and many outsiders from neighboring villages participated. This was common practice throughout Germany and probably stemmed from the attempt to protect the image of the local Nazis. Dansk was also part of the town council and advised the mayor's office to insure that the regime's instructions and dictates were carried out according to orders. Members of the SS and also Gestapo in plain clothes infiltrated most areas of employment and undertook spying, particularly on German employees who might not have been sympathetic to the regime. People today speak of "spies being everywhere" and they were often afraid to speak in public places for fear of being overheard by the SS. At all public events, including church services, black-suited SS were always present to report any wrongdoings to their superiors. In one such incident, Mr. Mauer, attending the Catholic church service, saw a Nazi taking notes on the sermon. As the priest began the sermon he noted the presence of the note-taking Nazi and said out loud, "You don't have to take notes here. Tomorrow morning, I'll send my sermon to you in writing. Here (in the church) there is nothing to watch."

The same Mr. Mauer, today an old, short man in his eighties with cataracts in his eyes, also told me of his encounter with the führer. Mauer was a civil servant in charge of the tax department. He had resisted joining the party until late in 1934, when he was compelled to join or lose his job. He went to the assistant mayor, who told him that he would have to pay 100 DM to join and told him to see the town führer, Dansk. He described his feelings of fear when he entered the room and recalled, "I was perspiring all over, although I had known Dansk since he was a child; there he was now, tall and towering in his black uniform and staring at me as if I were a stranger." Dansk knew of his anti-Nazi feelings and told him that "if he [the assistant mayor] had not said 100 DM already, I would have said 300 DM for you." Mauer paid down twenty-five marks and, although he was visited in his house several times by Dansk asking for the remainder of the money, he never paid more. After these incidents, Mauer kept quiet and never discussed his innermost feelings. He was one of the 600 party members in the town. Like him, many of the members were civil servants or teachers who were pressured to join the party by the threat of losing their positions. As Mauer said at the end of our discussion, "What could I have done, lose my job? How would I have supported my wife and two children? There were no other jobs here and nobody would ever have hired me if they knew I had refused to join the party. I would have been a marked man." Today, some of the Jewish survivors do not differentiate between the notorious Dansk family and a simple civil servant such as Mr. Mauer. Both are called "bad Nazis." The Dansk family came up often in our discussions and everyone agreed that they were the worst Nazis in the town. When I mentioned interviewing old Mr. Mauer, several people told me quickly, "Oh, Mauer, yes, he was also a bad Nazi."

From what can be gathered from respondents today, it would appear that the hard-core group was made up of all classes. As specified earlier, the first to join was the unemployed youth attracted by the promise of jobs. From the occupational descriptions of the majority, however, it appears that they were members of the middle class. They were shopkeepers, managers in the town factories, forestry officials and innkeepers. Dr. Ritter notes that people in managerial positions in the Miller factory were members but that some ordinary mill hands also joined the party. In addition, there were members who by local standards were clearly upper middle, or even upper, class, as with the more prosperous members of the Dansk family. These included the veterinarian, the doctor, and others described earlier as members of the SS.

This small community of Sonderburg was probably fairly representative of nationwide trends with respect to party membership. In 1939, there were five million members in a total German population of thirty million—or about 16 percent. By 1945, that figure had increased to eight million. Sonderburg was thus somewhat under the national average.

In terms of the total country, the middle and upper classes were overrepresented whereas the lower class was somewhat underrepresented.[5] In Sonderburg, too, impressionistic evidence suggests that the middle class was overrepresented: according to the census of 1933, 54 percent of the population was working class, 42.6 percent was middle class, and only 2.7 percent was upper class. Germany as a whole and Sonderburg as a case in point had a significantly higher proportion of working-class members as compared to the smaller middle class and the even smaller upper class. The majority of party members in the country and in Sonderburg were men.

Sarah A. Gordon and others have noted that the reasons for joining the party varied amongst the people. Parenthetically, it should be noted that the regime in its early days saw the party primarily as an elitist faction rather than as a mass movement. Accordingly, membership was opened in 1933 and then closed until 1937, when it was felt that having more members was desirable. Nevertheless, people who wanted to join always had influential friends who helped them gain entrance into the party.

It is highly likely that most early joiners were attracted by the promise of jobs and better economic and social conditions. For them and for later joiners, the anti-Semitic part of the Nazi program may have been of lesser importance. My impressions of the Sonderburg party members are that most of them joined the party for reasons other than hatred of the Jews. Gordon, analyzing P. Merkl, points to the "lower levels of anti-Semitism among rural or small town residents and residents of middle-sized towns." She notes that "the small percentage of anti-semitics from rural and middle-sized areas . . . indicates that they joined the Nazi party primarily for other reasons."[6] As for the levels of prejudice, Gordon concludes that in Merkl's sample of early Nazis almost 13 percent were raving fanatics and another 39 percent were moderately anti-Semitic. Roughly half the population was anti-Semitic and half was not.[7] Although my interview data did not contain any direct ways of measuring anti-Semitism, my impression is that less than half and perhaps closer to one-third of the Sonderburg population was anti-Semitic. People often mentioned the closeness that existed in this small community and the fact that members of both groups interacted on a day-to-day basis (see Chapters 3 and 6). Even Jewish respondents commented that before Hitler they had no real problems living amongst German Gentiles; only occasional incidents of anti-Semitism marred an otherwise comfortable style of life. Later, however, the specter of Nazism was to change those relations for both.

Other Aspects of Nazism

Other Nazi organizations in the town included the Hitler Youth and the Nazi Women's groups. The Hitler Youth recruited youngsters from the age of ten who were outfitted with a special uniform and who paraded in marches and rallies, attended classes in Hitlerism and the Nazi ideology, and were generally brainwashed. Some of their functions were recreational and included picnics and other outings, as well as supervised parties. Most schoolchildren were members of the Hitler Youth, though membership was not compulsory until March 1939, and their activities were supervised by adults who were members of the party. They were taught to think of themselves as superior to all others—they were to be the future of the country and Hitler himself was said to rely on them to maintain his great tradition. One man, now in his fifties, described to me his participation in the Hitler Youth: "For most of us, it was just fun, it was like a glorified Boy Scouts, we had lots of parties and outings, and sometimes we had classes, but many of us didn't pay much attention to those. We thought of ourselves as children having fun in an organization. We especially enjoyed the marches, all dressed up in our uniforms, marching through town and across the river, singing songs and accompanied by a brass band. I was eleven years old and having fun." Another person, Frau von Himmel, recalled that she, her husband, and their young son were on their way to church for Sunday mass when they were stopped by a neighbor and told that there was a Hitler Youth meeting that morning and they had better send young Eric there. Her husband said, "Some things they can't dictate, our church comes first and Eric comes with us." At the next meeting, young Eric was reprimanded for missing the previous session.

While more attention was paid to the boys in the Hitler Youth, the young girls were organized into the Bund Deutscher Mädchen (Organization of German Girls), or BDM, and participated in some of the same activities as their brothers. As females, however, they were taught the joys of Nazi motherhood and how to continue breeding the superior Aryan race. One program established by Himmler under the auspices of the SS was called the "Lebensborn" (fountain of life). It involved the selected breeding of Aryans: German girls of childbearing age were urged to volunteer to be impregnated by selected Aryan types. In Sonderburg this program was explained to girls of between seventeen and nineteen years of age, and they were urged to participate and to travel to a nearby center for the purpose. Apparently, the program on a nationwide basis was a failure. According to Frau Bilke, she and her friends were encouraged to participate at a meeting of the Organization of German Girls. They were offered financial assistance, gifts, compensation for all medical expenses, and a subsidy for the rearing of their children. Frau Bilke laughed even as she told the story and said, "We laughed at them even then, what a crazy idea. Most of us were dark-haired anyway, we might not even have had blond, blue-eyed children."

The Nazi ideology was taught in the school system and many, if not all, of the schoolteachers were Nazis. The denigration of the Jewish children in their classes will be described in Chapter 3. The teaching of Nazism was compulsory and it became a school subject just like history or geography. Propaganda from the regime, while slow in coming to a small community geographically removed from the centers of power, did nevertheless reach Sonderburg. Hitler's speeches were regularly reprinted in the local newspaper, and at rallies the speeches would be read out. In addition, loudspeakers would be set up in the market square whenever an important speech was broadcast since very few families owned radios. Pamphlets, brochures, and other Nazi literature were regularly distributed at meetings. Despite the propaganda, it appears that few people knew much about certain aspects of the ideology. The emphasis on the Aryan super race for example was vaguely heard about, but few people claimed to take it seriously. As one old and gray-haired lady noted, showing me a photo of herself taken at the age of twenty-two, "See my hair I had when I was young . . . almost black . . . we in Sonderburg weren't Aryans, most of us were dark-haired and dark-eyed." Clearly, the Aryan ideology meant very little to some of the people here.

From all accounts, the Nazis who survived the war returned to the Sonderburg area, and many not only received their old jobs but in some instances were given promotions as a result of distinguished war service.[8] Schoolteachers and others in public positions had to undergo denazification procedures before they could get their old jobs back. One of the main Nazis in the town, the second in command to the town führer, was a schoolteacher of some prominence. After the war, he, like others, was sent to a nearby town, where he had four weeks of instruction to unlearn the Nazi ways and then was given a test to determine, as one old man put it, "if one was human again." Many persons passed the test, including the schoolteacher, who received his job back and taught another generation of students. Another Nazi, who had held a minor administrative position connected with land usage and land surveys, was made a superintendent of land usage for the entire area, including several towns and villages. It was alleged by several people that the only way some of these officials were able to pass the denazification test was by bribing the examiners. When I asked why such people were given back positions of importance and even received promotions, a shrug of the shoulders was the reply. One person thought that the administration of government, the civil service, and the teaching profession were essential to restore order in the country and that there was no one else with the experience to undertake these responsibilities. "The country had to go on, who else could do these jobs? Me, I was only a chauffeur [and for a Jewish employer at that], I couldn't teach school." Frau Kurt, a shopkeeper's wife, made the same comment, "They all came back into their jobs after the war, we knew who they were; but life had to go on. We didn't inquire into who was and who wasn't anymore." It has often been alleged that many high positions, even prominent political positions, in West Germany today are filled by former Nazis and SS members.

Even in the small Sonderburg area, a microcosm of the larger society, former Nazis returned to assume important posts. Kurt Dansk, the leading Nazi in Sonderburg, died shortly after the war's end of natural causes.

The intriguing question that emerges from the growth of Nazism in Sonderburg and similar towns is why Nazism took hold so quickly in a community where ethnic relations between Jews and Gentiles had been of a fairly harmonious, accommodative nature. Most of the respondents from both groups ascribed this to the fact that Nazism appealed to the young, the unemployed and those who were basically "no good" anyway. Sonderburg, like any town, had its share of disenchanted youth due to the economic depression of the thirties. Hitler promised a rebounding economy and jobs for all. While I was unable to locate unemployment figures for Sonderburg during the late twenties and early thirties, respondents indicated that it was widespread. The unemployed (*Lumpen*, or hooligans) would have gravitated to Nazism simply because of its employment potential. Allen notes that in Thalberg many of the young men were unemployed and SA membership gave them something to do.[9] The fact that Nazism initially and increasingly was directed against the Jews would have meant little to those who embraced it for economic and social status reasons. The rush to join the party amongst the civil servants needs little explanation since many feared that they might lose their jobs even when joining was not compulsory. The Nazis used threats and intimidation to recruit new members. Herr Tiller recalls what happened to the volunteer fire brigade in Sonderburg:

> The fire brigade was composed of male volunteers who held other jobs. It was not in itself a paying position but it carried a considerable amount of prestige, and those within the brigade considered themselves to be very responsible and honest citizens. One night, all brigade members were called together, we thought it was to learn about a new piece of machinery. Actually, Dansk and Mueller [the town führer and his assistant] were there and they told us that "from now on, anybody who is not a member of the party can no longer serve in the fire brigade." Since I refused to join the party, I never went to another meeting of the brigade.

Professional people who joined the SS probably did so to enhance their status in the community. They were probably also imbued with the ideology and spirit of Nazism and saw in it a chance to recover the past glories of Germany. The veterinarian, for example, was described as a man who had always romanticized the German past; he was said to have always been extremely nationalistic, and he idolized Bismarck. Perhaps he saw in Hitler a reincarnation of his hero. Then again, in Sonderburg, as elsewhere, there were some people who had always hated the Jews. For them, the attractions of Nazism were even greater, for not only did the party make exuberant economic and social reform promises, it also legislated the exclusion and finally the elimination of the hated Jews from Aryan Germany.

Earlier, I cited a number of studies indicating that, by and large, the majority of Germans joined the Nazi party for reasons other than anti-Semitism. Allen's study of Thalberg, also a small community, was cited because he came essentially to the same conclusion. He notes that "Thalbergers were drawn to anti-semitism because they were drawn to Nazism, not the other way around. Many who voted Nazi simply ignored or rationalized the anti-semitism of the party, just as they ignored other unpleasant aspects of the Nazi movement." In Thalberg, there were 120 Jews out of a total population of 10,000 (in 1930) and "social discrimination against Jews was practically non-existent. Jews were integrated along class lines . . . yet abstract anti-semitism in the form of jokes or expressions of generalized distaste was prevalent. . . . If Nazi anti-semitism held any appeal for the townspeople, it was in highly abstract form, as a remote theory unconnected with daily encounters with real Jews in Thalberg."[10] In Sonderburg, as later chapters will emphasize, there was more social anti-Semitism than Allen describes for Thalberg, but his general conclusion applies. By and large the majority of Nazi party members, though probably not the hard-core SA and SS members, were drawn to Nazism for other reasons. Allen's reasons concur with my findings, including the depression, the party's platform to restore the economy, the encouragement of class antagonisms, the resurgent nationalism, and the very active political campaigning by the party. "In short, the NSDAP [the party] succeeded in being all things to all men."[11]

Nazi Electoral Strength in Sonderburg

I have estimated party membership in Sonderburg at about 15 percent of the population by the mid- to the late thirties. This percentage includes about a hundred men, or 2 percent, who were hard-core Nazis; most of them were either members of the SA or the SS.

The hard core was composed of men like Dansk who were completely committed to the ideology of Nazism. Some joiners, like the civil servants, feared either job loss or seized the opportunity of joining the party for personal gain, such as promotions and enhanced security. Others were attracted by the anti-Semitism of Nazism. This leaves a remaining 85 percent of the population, many of whom even today claim that they had little, if anything, to do with Nazism. One measure of their feelings about Nazism is revealed in electoral results. How many voted for the party in the last general election of 1933 or those prior to 1933? Furthermore, how does Sonderburg compare with the national results, as well as with the other small towns?

In the election of November 6, 1932, the party took 33.1 percent of the total vote, which was enough to have Hitler appointed chancellor on January 30, 1933. In the subsequent election of March 5, 1933, the party increased its support to 43.9 percent but was still short of an overall majority. Richard Hamilton's recently published work, *Who Voted for Hitler*, sheds new light on these and other results.[12] He notes that the party's main attraction for those disenchanted with the vagaries of the Weimar Republic in the urban areas of the country was to counteract the fear of Marxism, particularly since the Communist party had substantial strength in the larger cities. For rural areas, promised improvement was the major attraction: "the National Socialists spoke the key words, 'debt relief,' when no one else was doing so. As the depression worsened, the parties of the local notables shifted to the right, rejecting any suggestion of relief. But, for the first time, a plausible alternative was present and actively appealing to the rural voters."[13] Hamilton's figures show that the Protestant countryside gave the Nazi party its most substantial electoral support, reaching in some rural districts to well over 70 percent of the vote. In Germany's largest cities, support for the party (in 1932) ranged from a low of 20 percent (Dortmund) to a high of 46 percent. Hamilton estimates that "somewhere between 20–25 percent of the total population would be contained in rural Protestant areas. Not all of these persons . . . would be farmers. Many of the villages and small towns' populations engaged in trade and commerce were, of course, directly dependent on agriculture. The NSDAP . . . gained its greatest electoral successes within this context."[14]

Sonderburg was predominantly Protestant (64 percent Protestant and 32 percent Catholic), but it was less dependent on agriculture than some other rural areas since nearly half or 46 percent of its labor force was engaged in industrial and wage labor as compared to only 9 percent in agriculture. Lesser dependence on agriculture, as well as a fairly substantial Catholic population, one third of the town's total population, may be factors that influenced electoral results in Sonderburg. Table 1 (page 45) indicates the results of elections held between May, 1924, and March, 1933, for Sonderburg as compared to nationwide results. The figures reveal that there was always substantial support for those parties that leaned toward either a centrist or slightly left orientation as demonstrated by the results for the Social Democratic party (SPD) in Sonderburg, as well as nationally. Zentrum, a centrist Catholic party, also regularly gathered about one fifth of the vote (somewhat less than the actual number of Catholics in the population). Zentrum's support in Sonderburg was always substantially higher than its nationwide share of the electorate. The Communist share of the vote in Sonderburg was always lower than national average except for the election of 1930 when it was identical. The DDP, or German Democratic Party, a liberal-centrist group, began with some support in Sonderburg but from 1930 onward it received no support. Another right-wing, conservative party, the DNVP—which also contained an anti-Semitic faction—fared substantially less well in Sonderburg than in the nation and received no support at all in 1933. By then, however, earlier voters of the right-wing DNVP were probably voting for the Nazis.

Another way of examining these figures is to classify them into parties of the right and parties of the center-left. This technique has its dangers, however, since most political parties in the Weimar Republic were segmented into different groups and factions. Their ideologies and boundaries shifted with the political tides and with the necessity of forming political coalitions.[15] Nevertheless, as gross indicator of political ideologies, the exercise yields some interesting results as Table 2 (page 46) indicates:

Thus, from 1924 to 1930, more persons in Sonderburg voted for parties of the center-left than for those on the right-wing end of the political spectrum. From the high point in December 1924, the differences began to get smaller. By 1930 only 13 percent separated the right from the left, and by 1933 that trend was completely reversed and there were then more right-wing than left-wing voters. What is worth noting is that in the earlier years Sonderburgers voted left-center more than did the nation as a whole, but from May 1928 to 1933, votes of the left were essentially comparable to the nationwide figures. Conversely, for the earlier years, fewer Sonderburgers voted for the right as compared to the national figures. This difference is

TABLE 1—Electoral Results

	May 1924		Dec. 1924		May 1928		Sept. 1930		March 1933	
	Sond.	Nation-wide	Sond.	Nation-wide	Sond.	Nation-wide	Sond.	Nation-wide	Sond.	Nation-wide
SPD—Social Democratic Party	20.8	20.5	20	26	28.5	29.8	20.8	24.5	17.4	18.3
KPD—Communists	3.7	12.6	3.6	9	2.2	10.6	13.1	13.1	5.6	12.3
Zentrum—Catholic middle	23	13.4	24.3	13.6	18.8	12.1	20.8	11.8	18.8	11.3
DDP—Left Liberal Center	12.2	5.7	15	6.3	7.3	4.9		3.8		0.8
DVP—Right Liberal Laissez-faire	30	9.2	29	10.1	22	8.7	7.3	4.5	8	1.1
DNVP—Conservatives Right Wing, anti-Semitic	4.9	19.5	6.8	20.5	3.4	14.2	2	7		8
Others	2.1	12.6	1	11.5	15.2	17.1	25.2*	17	6.6	4.3
NSDAP—Nazi Party		6.5		3	1.4	2.6	7.1	18.3	42	43.9
Total	98.8**	100	99.7	100	98.8	100	100	100	98.4	100
Participation	75.9	77.4	67.5	78.8	69.6	75.5	81.5	82	89.1	88.7

*Many splinter parties
**Do not add to 100 percent because of rounding
Source: Sonderburg figures, *Statistik des Deutschen Reiches*, vol. 451. Nationwide figures, Hamilton, p. 476.

TABLE 2—Voting Trends

	Center Left	Nationwide	Right	Nationwide	Difference
May 1924	59.7 (SPD, KPD, Zent, DDP)	52.2	37 (DVP, DNVP, other)	47	left-right 22.7
December 1924	62.9	55	36.8	45.1	26
May 1928	56.8	57.4	42 (including unknown splinter parties)	42.6	14.8
September 1930	54.7	53.2	41.6	46.8	13.1
1933	43.2 (SPD, KPD, DSP, Zent)	42.7	55.2 (DVP, NAZI Kampffront)	57.3	Right-Left 2.1

also noted in the last election of 1933 where fewer Sonderburgers voted for the right but about the same numbers voted for the Nazi party as did those nationally.

What these trends indicate is that there was a significant centrist-left tradition in this community. The Nazi party did not make very substantial inroads into this tradition since considerably less than half of the electorate voted for it even in 1933. This is particularly noteworthy since in many small towns and rural communities, the vote for the Nazi party was more than 50 percent, reaching as high as 80–100 percent in some areas. For example in Thalberg, as described by Allen, only 27.5 percent voted toward the center-left in 1933 as compared to 43.2 percent in Sonderburg.[16] Similarly, the Nazi party in 1930 and 1933 reached 28.2 percent and 62.7 percent respectively. In Sonderburg for the same years, the figures of 7 percent and 42 percent showed considerably less support for the Nazi party. (Thalberg had fewer Catholics and the Nazi party was particularly active in its organization there.) But as noted earlier, the combination of some (one third) Catholicism, nondependence on agriculture, and a tradition of voting for left-centrist political parties in earlier times are some of the factors that may account for these results. We may also speculate, in the absence of motivational data, that in view of these factors, the people who did turn to the right, and more specifically to the Nazi party in the thirties, did so for reasons other than anti-Semitism.

On the other hand, it should also be emphasized that *although fewer Sonderburgers than other rural people voted for Nazism*, a very substantial 42 percent did so, and this figure is just slightly below the nationwide results for 1933 of 44 percent. Hamilton notes that after 1930, there was "a flow to the radical right. . . ."[17] This flow is also reflected in the voting patterns for the right in Sonderburg, when in 1933, 55.2 percent voted for the right-wing parties.

Do these voting patterns add anything to our understanding of the dynamics of Nazism in Sonderburg? In the first instance, they strengthen the impressionistic reconstruction of the Nazi period presented by the living respondents in this study. Both Gentile and Jewish respondents agreed that there were probably no more than about 600 party members in Sonderburg throughout the Nazi period. This figure is 15 percent of the total population of 4,000. The electoral results show that an additional 500 members of the voting population cast their ballots for the Nazi party in 1933 since the vote in numbers was exactly 1,100. It may be concluded therefore that Sonderburg was not an especially vital stronghold of Nazism.

These results also lend more credence to the Gentile respondents who claimed that they had little, if anything, to do with Nazism. In fact, 58 percent did not even vote for its candidates.

Numbers alone do not, however, reduce the fear and terror that Jews had to contend with as described in Chapter 3. One woman commented on the small numbers but added, "There weren't really that many, but those 100 or so were terrible." It should also be noted here (but will be discussed more fully in later chapters) that both the SA and the SS even in Sonderburg were often reinforced by members from neighboring communities. Reinforcements were called in particularly for public events such as marches and rallies so that these groups always appeared to be more numerous than they actually were in any one community. In Chapters 3 and 4, the population of Sonderburg is classified into two small groups at the polar ends of a continuum. At one end are about 100 confirmed Nazis, at the other, about an equal number of people who helped Jews, and the remainder formed a passive majority. Who voted for the Nazis in Sonderburg? Obviously the Nazi party members and another 500 or so who belonged to the passive majority. This leaves about 1,500 persons of voting age. About a hundred of them not only helped Jews but probably did not vote for the party either. There were then about 1,400 persons, members of the passive majority, whose only noteworthy act was not to vote for the Nazi party.

Today, people laugh as they recount aspects of Nazism which they claim amused them even then. It may well be that it is only in retrospect that they laugh about having had fun in the Hitler Youth or having been born with black instead of blond hair. The implication that Nazism was laughable comes with the hindsight of forty or more years, but at the time Nazi messages were probably well received and perhaps the very woman who can laugh today about having had black hair wished at the time that she conformed more closely to the Aryan physical type. Gentiles today describe the terrible fear under which they and their neighbors lived. They were in terror of the SA and the SS, whose spies were everywhere and whose main function was to seek out dissident Germans. These dissidents were often picked up and detained for the most minor offenses. When one of my respondents said "we were all caught under a net," he meant that very literally; few, if any, were able to escape. The Jews however, lived under even more perilous conditions. Merely locking their doors against Nazi intruders or keeping their mouths shut while publicly lauding the regime would not have saved them from the real terrors of death in the camps or even their enforced departure from a country that they had considered their own for centuries. Some Germans may have privately laughed about the silliness of the Aryan ideology and other aspects of Nazism, but they knew that if they did not challenge it or any other part of the regime, they would be safe. The Jews had no such recourse to safety.

A group of Sonderburg teenagers in 1918, enjoying an excursion. Both Jews and Gentiles are in the group.

3

ETHNIC RELATIONS BETWEEN JEWS AND GENTILES BEFORE 1933

A brief overview of the history of Sonderburg reveals that Jews had lived there for many centuries. Even though the group was never large, its presence in the community was nevertheless felt because of its economic influence. In this chapter, I will examine in more detail the nature of the Jewish-Gentile relationship before 1933 in order to see how these two ethnic groups lived in a state of stable accommodation to each other.

Sonderburg's remaining Jews and Germans agree that life before the Nazis in Sonderburg was good. The community was relatively prosperous and, although there was unemployment during the 1920s and early 1930s, on the whole the social and economic life of the community functioned smoothly. The town was characterized by friendliness and harmony, and, while there were the usual frictions that characterize any small town, no friction existed between Jews and Gentiles. Although there is a hint of condescension in German testimony today—their attitude is that "our Jews were good people, they never gave us any trouble"—there is no evidence of any overt hostility between the groups at that time. On the other hand, the relationship was never more than one of accommodation. True assimilation never existed.

The closest associations between the two groups took place in the work place or in business areas. Gentiles routinely patronized Jewish shops, and the owners depended on this trade to remain in business. Jewish families were well known, and, as in any small town, customers would shop, chat, and often inquire about the shopkeepers' families: "How are the children?" "Is your mother-in-law recovering from her illness?" "How is your son doing in the city?" In both communities major events such as births, marriages, deaths, and school graduations were broadcast to all. The gossips were equally active in both communities and news about each other's personal activities spread quickly. Since both communities were stratified by class (although the majority of Jews were middle class), news and activities were more readily known within the same class levels. But the town was small enough so that major events or crises in the lives of individuals within any class were widely known throughout the community. A Jewish or a Gentile marriage was newsworthy, and the kinship connections of both bride and groom were actively discussed: "Young Lisl married Georg Hahn; you know his family from Starkerheim—he's the son of old Eric, the butcher, and his mother came from Frankfurt," and so on. Such discussions would take place in both communities regardless of whether the incident involved a Jewish or a Gentile family. Jews and Gentiles in Sonderburg led a typical small-town existence and events both within and between the two groups became public knowledge fairly quickly.

Of the five largest employers, two were Jewish firms; in one case, the Jewish-owned mill employed hundreds of Gentile workers—as many as 20 percent of the working adult labor force. In a very real sense, the Gentile community depended on Jews for employment and for retail goods. Likewise, Jews depended on Gentiles for either a labor force or a retail market. The situation can perhaps best be described as one of mutual, harmonious dependency.

Frau Krammer's history provides a case in point. She is today a widowed pensioner in her seventies. Her very modest old-age pension is supplemented by a drink business which she conducts out of her home, selling beer, wine and soft drinks at a small profit, usually to the after-hour trade. Her husband was a minor official at the railroad for most of his life, and both came from working-class backgrounds. Her parents had owned a small farm on the outskirts of the city, and because the family worked industriously, they were fairly comfortable financially and "there was always a little extra for the children at Christmas time." Her earliest recollections of Jews were of her father regularly selling farm produce—primarily vegetables, chickens and eggs— to Jewish middlemen, who in turn sold the goods to retail shops in town. Their relationship was always good: "Nobody ever cheated us and the Jew Mexheim [the middleman] always paid good prices to us." As a young girl leaving school, she joined the Miller factory as a knitter and worked there for fourteen years, until the birth of her second child. In 1873 her grandmother had been the first knitter employed at the mill, and her mother also worked there, as did her two aunts and her brother, making Frau Krammer the third generation to work for the Jewish-owned mill. She says the Millers were good to work for as they paid good wages; she also describes them as wonderful people who took special care of their workers and were on a first-name basis with all of them. In particular, the owner's wife, Frau Miller, was especially kind to everyone. When Frau Krammer had her first child, Frau Miller sent hot meals to her home for fourteen days and a cleaning woman for three weeks. Frau Krammer's brother received a grant of money and a handsome radio when he retired from the firm after forty years of service.

She recalls how she and her mother purchased dry goods in the Mandels' store and how Frau Mandel always gave them a bit of extra cloth; she did this for all her good customers. The Jewish stores "were the best in town—everything could be bought there." When she was young, she went to school with the two children from the Heyman family and was fairly friendly with them. They would sometimes visit each other's homes and would often play together after school. Today, Frau Krammer speaks with affection about "our Jews," and says she never could understand what Hitler had against them. They did so much for the Sonderburg community by contributing to charity and by creating work: "almost everybody depended on them for employment." However, Frau Krammer had no real social ties with Jewish families. As her story shows, aside from the childhood connections, the ties for her occurred only in the business and employment area. The main reason was the barrier between the working class and the majority of the Jews. She was, and still is, a working-class person whereas most of the Jews were, and were perceived to be, the middle-class *bessere Leute* (better class of people).

Herr Tiller is another example of a working-class Gentile who had close occupational ties with several Jewish families but no particular ties of friendship. Upon leaving school, he was employed in the Kahn department store as Herr Kahn's personal chauffeur. The Kahns owned one of the few cars to appear in Sonderburg shortly after World War I. His Jewish boss was always considerate. Wherever he drove him, a short distance out of town or on a vacation to Switzerland or France, Tiller was treated as one of the family. He ate at the same table with the Kahn family (few Jews observed the Orthodox dietary laws) and his personal expenses were covered. He, too, had grown up with Jewish boys and says today that he has never had anything against the Jews: "They were decent people and very good to work for." In noting how dependent many Gentiles were on Jewish employment, he borrows the words of an old saying, "Der, der wer mich ernährt hatte, dem habe ich nichts dagegen" (I have nothing against the person who supported me). Even today he calls Herr Kahn, long deceased, "der Chef—the boss," and he makes much of the equality of their relationship although Kahn was "a very rich man" and "I was only his chauffeur." Herr Tiller also served as a chauffeur for various occasions, and much of his private employment was by Jews who hired him to drive wedding parties, or to take them to bar mitzvahs in other towns. Again, he says, he was always treated courteously and paid well. His older brother also worked in the Kahn department store as a clerk for over twenty years. Both brothers left their Jewish employ when the store was forced to close. Today, Herr Tiller says that the best thing that happened after the war was the payment of reparations to some Jews for their lost businesses and properties. "It was a shame, what they had to sell for; Schmidt, the new owner of the Kahn department store, got it for almost nothing. But after the war, he was forced to pay the market value of the store to the Kahns." Herr Tiller had a healthy respect for Jewish entrepreneurial skills and felt that Jews always worked extremely hard.

Although most interaction occurred during business and employment hours, close friendships did emerge at two levels. Close friendships were formed in school, that is, primary and secondary school. The town had only one public high school so all children automatically attended it. Friendships were facilitated by age grading so that sometimes there would only be one Jewish child of a certain age and his playmates automatically would be Gentile children. There were never enough Jewish children at any one age level for them to form special or exclusive groups. In another section of this book, John Miller notes that there was only one Jewish boy of his age and they did not much care for each other, so both played with Gentiles instead. Given the small size of the community, friendships begun in primary school were continued into high school and on into adulthood—until they were broken by the advent of the Hitler era. Children were somewhat more supervised in those times; nevertheless, they visited each other's home after school. A favorite pastime (since there were no movies in Sonderburg and the age of television had not begun) involved groups of school-age children who formed what were called Wandergruppen, that is, excursion groups. It is sometimes assumed that the Wandergruppen were invented by the Nazis as a youth pastime, but clearly such groups had appeared much earlier as a form of leisure activity for teen-agers, including Jewish teen-agers. They would set off for the woods or on long-distance hikes into the mountains that surround the River Valley. The older high school students would often spend the summer holidays by taking longer excursions, and Jewish playmates were sometimes included. After high school, the young people of wealthier families were sent away to further their education, and friendships became somewhat disrupted since some never returned to Sonderburg and made new friends elsewhere. But for those who remained in the community to earn their livelihood, the friendships continued. During the last high school years, when students began dating, most of the Jewish young people had Gentile boyfriends and girlfriends as will be seen in greater detail at the end of this chapter.

Friendships also developed at the neighborhood level. Despite the fact that Sonderburg was a town of only 4,000 inhabitants, it had some distinct neighborhood clusters. One such neighborhood was on Grossestrasse (Main Street), where most of the shops were located. The shop owners usually lived in the same building, with the shop occupying the lower level and the family quarters the upstairs. Occasionally, the living quarters would be behind the shop. Many of the Jewish shopkeepers lived on Grossestrasse, or on small streets that led into it, and they were surrounded by Gentile neighbors. Close attachments between the women developed quite naturally. Social patterns in those times did not usually involve couples visiting each other's homes in the evening. It was more common for women to get together during the late afternoon for coffee and cake. Mrs. Frankel, today in her eighties, recalls the gatherings that took place even in her mother's time, around the turn of the century and earlier. "My mother had many friends, ladies who came to the house and they had Kaffeeklatsch, ten or twelve or so; the cakes came from the Konditorei [pastry shop] in Kreuzen."

Almost all of Mrs. Frankel's friends were Gentiles. She particularly remembers a Kaffeeklatsch friend whose wedding she was invited to attend. This took place just before World War I. "She married an officer and I was invited to the wedding. Boy, that was a wedding and I was the only Jewish girl there." At her own wedding in 1920, "many Gentile friends came." Thus friendships were continued between the two groups through the pattern of Jewish and Gentile women who lived nearby regularly visiting each other. Afternoon coffee a couple of times a week where conversation and gossip were exchanged was a regular feature of social life.

The men followed a similar pattern, but it involved visiting taverns or cafes during the early evening, shortly after the light evening meal (the main meal was eaten at midday). They would remain there for a few hours and then return home around nine or ten o'clock. Men gathered during the evenings primarily to play cards and to drink beer or wine with each other. This custom was so ritualized that each particular group would have its own table—the *Stammtisch*—reserved for it at the cafe or tavern. As men arrived, a place was made for them at their *Stammtisch*, where the main activity was card playing. These male groups were completely integrated, and Jewish men regularly met and played cards with Gentile friends. Those friends were occasionally work mates or simply people one met at the same *Stammtisch*. Thus, Mr. Abraham regularly played with the tailor, one of the grocers, and one of the shoe-store owners, all Gentiles. Mr. Martin, a Jewish inhabitant of a small village on the outskirts of Sonderburg, remembers that one of his card-playing mates was already in 1932 a member of the Nazi party and destined to become an important official; until early 1933, they were still playing cards together! However, this stopped within days of Hitler's appointment as chancellor in January 1933.

Thus, men spent their leisure hours with other men and women did the same. Only mixed-sex visiting did not often take place—perhaps a reflection of an older, nineteenth-century, pattern, in which male and female activities were not considered to have the same prestige. In any event, drinking and card playing was the activity of men, coffee parties were the main social activity of women, and both Gentiles and Jews took part in each. Class divisions were fairly strictly observed. Although the men's tavern pattern was somewhat more egalitarian than the women's get-togethers, the

group that formed each *Stammtisch* was by and large of similar
class status. The women who met together were members of the
upper middle and upper class. Mrs. Frankel says that her parents
were very well off since her father was a storekeeper and, in a sense,
a "banker—he lent money to the farmers." Both her parents had
gone to school in larger cities and were well educated; consequently
they were "very much respected by everybody." Her mother's
friends included a few Jewish women, but most were Gentile from
the same class level. Mrs. Frankel's mother enjoyed her Gentile
upper-class friends, but this would have been about the middle of
the nineteenth century. By the turn of the century or thereabouts,
attitudes appeared to have hardened. John Miller, for instance notes,
that the rise in anti-Semitism prior to World War I prevented his
parents from joining in social activities.

Both Jewish and Gentile respondents agreed that relations between the two groups were entirely normal and cordial. "We all
lived together just as in any small town, we were all the same kinds
of people" were comments often made by members of both groups.
It might be supposed that the outstanding difference between them
was in the sphere of religion, but even here there was a considerable
amount of sharing. For example, Gentile children and even adults
participated in the important Jewish holidays; at every Passover,
matzoth, or wafers of unleavened bread, were routinely given out
to non-Jewish children and even their parents. One Gentile man
recalled that in his youth he would look forward to Passover because
he had developed a fondness for matzoth. Some Gentiles, particularly children, attended the synagogue on festive occasions, and
there were even a few reported cases of Gentiles taking part in the
bar mitzvah ceremony for a Jewish boy; a few of the Jewish men
interviewed remembered receiving gifts from their Gentile friends
on that occasion. One Gentile woman remembered that when her
two Jewish friends received money at Hanukkah, the Festival of
Lights, she too was given some so as not to feel left out. Several of
the Jews reported that they always participated in the Christmas
festivities of their Christian friends. Decorating the tree was an
activity in which Jewish friends helped and one woman recalls that
she knew more traditional Christmas songs than Hebrew or Jewish
ones. Much of this shared activity took place among members of
the younger generation, yet it was undertaken with the full consent
of their families. Minna, for example, said that "often one or two
of my Gentile friends would be invited to stay for Friday night
dinner, a night when Jewish families celebrated the beginning of

the Sabbath and usually cooked an elaborate meal." She noted that these were often happy occasions and that her parents particularly enjoyed the presence of her friends. In fact, in commenting on these shared experiences, several persons noted that the division between Protestants and Catholics in the town was far more rigid than that between either of these groups and the Jews.[1] Thus, even though the two groups were of different religions, social relations were at times enhanced rather than hindered by them since children, especially, participated in each other's rituals. There were then many important contacts between Jews and Gentiles. These ties of association were, on the whole, affected by the social class standing of the two groups. For working-class Gentiles, contacts with the more middle-class Jews were made in the work place and in retail trade, whereas actual friendships occurred more often between the Jews and Gentiles of middle-class standing.

Despite the many and varied contacts between Jews and Gentiles, important areas of social life were closed to the Jews regardless of their wealth or position. For instance, they were barred from the Casino club—a private social, recreational, and athletic club that charged a membership fee and was entitled to restrict its membership. Founded in the late nineteenth century, it drew its members primarily from the social elite of Sonderburg and neighboring towns, that is to say, the two wealthy Gentile factory owners, and others of the Gentile middle-class who could afford the fee. The club's unwritten but accepted policy had always been not to admit Jewish members, regardless of their wealth or class standing. Thus the Millers, the wealthiest family in the entire area, were denied membership despite their many efforts to join. Mrs. Frankel, today a woman in her late eighties and my oldest Jewish respondent, remembers that in her youth, around the turn of the century, and even earlier when her parents were young, the Casino club had been out of bounds to Jews. This longstanding exclusionist policy was probably introduced in the mid- or late nineteenth century, when anti-Semitism was running high in Germany. It certainly predated the Hitler period by many years.

Sonderburg also had an intellectual or literary society to which schoolteachers, advanced students, the mayor, affluent Gentiles, and so-called pseudointellectuals belonged. Jews were not admitted to this circle. Even the highly educated and sophisticated senior members of the Miller family were excluded. However, Mr. Hilfer, Minna's father, did belong to the literary society during the twenties. An exception was probably made for him because of his reputation as a man of letters and as a poet. He was regularly asked to read his poetry at literary society meetings. He was also a founding member of a choral group that aside from him comprised only Gentiles. He was, however, the only Jew to participate in these activities, no doubt because he was perceived by all to be a very refined and cultured person.

Sonderburg also had a tennis club, from which Jews were barred. It was run by the Women's Organization, a group of upper-middle and upper-class Gentile women who organized a number of recreational and charitable events. This same group sponsored Red Cross fund-raising activities, and wealthy Jewish women like Mrs. Miller were invited to contribute their money and their energy despite their exclusion from the purely social and recreational functions of the organization. Mrs. Miller held charity and Red Cross meetings in her home, and she attended such meetings in the homes of upper-class Gentile women, but a more intimate form of social contact between them never formed. Her services as both a major financial contributor and tireless worker for charitable causes were well known and admired but did not give her entree into social life. Today, her children still comment on her disappointment in not being fully admitted into upper-class Gentile society, and her husband (according to a few of the Jewish respondents, including some relations) was said to have tried all sorts of subtle ways in which to gain membership into exclusive Gentile circles, but without any real success.

The irony of this situation was that some of the same women who visited Jewish women's houses for Kaffeeklatsch also attended the more formal Women's Organization, which practiced anti-Semitic exclusionism. Another elite family, a Gentile factory owner and his Jewish-born wife (one of the very few mixed marriages and the only mixed couple who remained in Sonderburg), was also isolated from these intellectual and athletic circles. These exclusionist policies must have started well before World War I because John Miller remembers that, around the turn of the century, his grandparents did belong to these circles, but "then they didn't anymore; the German anti-Semitism and the rise in nationalist feelings isolated them, though under regular circumstances, they would have been part of the social life of the town."

Thus well before the Hitler period, there was some anti-Semitism in Sonderburg. A famous anti-Semitic incident took place in the early 1920s, after the assassination of Walter Rathenau, a Jew who served as the foreign minister of the Weimar Republic.[2] During the night after the assassination, someone painted three large swastikas in tar all over the Miller house. Despite investigation, the culprits were never found.

Other seemingly isolated incidents took place in school. A number of the Jewish respondents mentioned that Jewish children were subjected to insulting name-calling: they were called "Christ killer" or "dirty Jew," particularly whenever fights and arguments broke out over other issues. As one of the younger Millers put it, "Being Jewish set up certain tensions, I guess, even early. We were a very small minority of Jewish children and sometimes we were called names or beat up by other kids—it emerged very erratically but it was there." John Miller was the only Jew in his grade and, he recalls, "I wasn't particularly popular or unpopular; I had a number of friends and I had no social problems until later. But I became conscious as time went on, especially after a beating by a few kids, and I came home to hear, 'That is typically German to jump on somebody,' and then I said to myself, 'What, am I not German?' I experienced a crisis of identity and did not know how to handle it. I knew that my father was active in politics and was more or less considered an important man, but then I got put down, couldn't understand it, and had no recourse of any kind."

Several of the Gentiles interviewed also remember these incidents, but they tend to dismiss them as not serious—the kind of bantering and fighting that all children enjoy. Two Jewish respondents recall that they were sometimes excluded from the social activities of other children, but they seem to have been in the minority. Most Jews recall their childhood as being without unfortunate incidents. In one amusing interview, a woman complained that she was once excluded from a Wandergruppe trip; her brother quickly interjected, "But that was because of your nasty temperament." During the 1920s and earlier, relations between the two groups at school were generally good despite a few name-calling incidents, but a dramatic change took place in the school system during the early 1930s, when instances of exclusion and anti-Semitism markedly increased. The Miller family had eight children, and while the four older ones report no problems in school, the four youngest say that their school experiences were decidedly unpleasant. John remembers that, even in early 1933, his comments in school were reported to the SS: "The day after the Reichstag [parliament] burned, I, like a dumb kid, said in school, 'That wasn't a communist that burnt it.' One hour later I went home for lunch and there was an SS man at the door who said to my father, 'Mr. Miller, your son said such and so at school. Give me your German flag,' which was black, red and gold. He returned later with a gun to collect it and frightened the hell out of all of us, particularly me for having said it was the Nazis themselves who had set fire to the Reichstag. This was said among fourteen-year-old kids and I was reported; I think I know who did it but it made no difference, as I was by then already isolated." John's younger sister recalls that two of her teachers were avowed Nazis and that one of them led the attack on her home during Kristallnacht. She said that her classmates made comments to her Gentile friends such as "How can you play with Jews?" In the classroom, the Gentile children all stood up to salute "Heil Hitler" while the Jewish children remained seated, feeling awkward and embarrassed. She, too, recalls feeling completely isolated in school and after hours as well.

Another source of tension in school was the increased teaching of Aryan Nazi ideology. Lectures on Nazism were given regularly since the early thirties and stereotypic descriptions of "inferior" non-Aryans, mainly Jews, were part of these lessons. Jews were described as individuals having long, hooked noses, wearing black gabardine coats, and carrying peddler packs on their backs, the image being that of the East European peddler Jew. Irmgard, a Gentile woman who was a schoolgirl at the time, says that none of the children recognized such an image since the Jews in their community looked, dressed and acted just like Germans—the stereotype East European Jew was completely foreign to them. She says that kids would frequently laugh and snigger during those lessons and that nobody would take them very seriously. On the other hand, the Jewish children in the class were forced to endure these lessons, and Hildegard, a Jewish woman who was also a schoolgirl then, recalls how terrible it made her feel. She also remembers that later, in the mid-thirties, when she was just about to graduate from high school, the local Nazi organization urged her and other female schoolmates to join the Aryan program, which involved registering to become the mothers of Aryan children by mating with selected "pure Aryan" men. She says that none of the girls in Sonderburg volunteered for this program and that, in fact, they laughed at it. The impression given by Jewish and Gentile repondents who were of school age at the time is that the entire Aryan program and its ideology as taught in the schools and at Hitler Youth was something of a joke. Nevertheless, all Gentile teen-agers in the community did belong to the Hitler Youth, but for them it was a fun type of activity. While the Gentile youths enjoyed the marches, drills, uniforms, and silly school lectures, the pain these activities inflicted on their Jewish schoolmates apparently went unnoticed.

Intermarriage

When two groups live together in a small, fairly harmonious, and mutually dependent community, one would expect the relationship between them to be strengthened by intermarriage. However, contrary to nationwide trends in the twentieth century, intermarriage very rarely occurred in Sonderburg.

The twentieth century brought a very rapid increase in the number of mixed marriages in Germany. Between 1910 and 1929, the number of Jews marrying non-Jews rose from 8 percent to 23 percent. Mixed marriages were most common in large cities—where one out of every three Jews was marrying outside the faith—because "the ease of social intercourse undermined the traditional authority of religious and social caste lines."[3] In Berlin, which had almost one-third of the overall Jewish population, the rate of intermarriage was the highest. Jews were in part motivated to intermarry because of their need to "assimilate" into German society. In large cities, this need was stronger than in rural areas, where ethnic bonds were stronger; young people, free from a lot of tradition and parental teaching, mingled freely with members of the other faiths at university and at their place of employment. The opportunity existed to meet age mates or peers from other groups. Intermarriage was encouraged by the nineteenth-century reform movement among Jews, who relinquished traditional Orthodox beliefs in their attempt to modernize their faith and assimilate into German society.

In Sonderburg during the 1920s and early 1930s, only three intermarriages occurred. Two were between Jewish men and non-Jewish women, and each couple had met in a large city. Both women were from other towns in Germany, and both left the Protestant religion for Judaism upon marriage. There was also the daughter of a Jewish family who met a Protestant man in a large city, converted to Protestantism, married him and moved away. One prominent Gentile businessman, a factory owner, married a Jewish woman in 1920, but she did not come from Sonderburg. In the previous generation, between 1900 and 1920, only one marriage between a Jewish woman and a Gentile man is known to have taken place, and both persons lived in a neighboring village, not in Sonderburg proper.

Thus, there were only a few intermarriages, and none occurred between men and women who had been born and raised in Sonderburg. Almost all of the Jewish respondents interviewed for this study had, however, gone out with or dated non-Jewish persons in their youth and early adulthood. One woman kept company with a non-Jew from grade school to the end of high school, when she left the community in search of further opportunity in a larger city. They had gone everywhere together and had been well known in both groups as a "pair." They never married, supposedly for personal reasons, but the man's mother was strongly anti-Semitic and would frequently take her son to task for his defiance in going out with a "Jew person." A Jewish man said he had regularly gone out with Gentile girls, but it had never occurred to him that he might ever marry one—"It just wasn't done here." Another male respondent told a similar story, and several of the women respondents had Gentile boyfriends. In three cases, the parents of the Jewish partner in a dating relationship objected to the marriage. One woman's parents, who tried to dissuade her from marrying her non-Jewish boyfriend, had themselves been victims of earlier parental pressure. Both parents had been in "out-faith" relationships in their youth, and in both instances, it had been the Jewish family that objected to intermarriage. Today, this woman bitterly recounts the unhappy marriage of her parents, who were wed on the rebound from their Gentile sweethearts. She maintains that her Gentile boyfriend could not leave Germany at the time of her emigration to the United States; had historical circumstances not intervened, they might have married each other. On the whole, there was a considerable amount of mixed friendship and dating among older teen-agers and younger adults. Many of these ties developed from earlier school relationships, but none led to marriage. The feeling among people today is that it was mainly the Jewish parents and grandparents who objected to intermarriage and inculcated these feelings into their children. Most people say that, although it was never specifically discussed in the home, they were nevertheless expected to marry someone Jewish. One woman tells of her older brother's engagement to a Gentile woman in Frankfurt; when her brother called home with the news, their father told the rest of the family that "Arthur is marrying a Gentile, *but* she is a good girl"—the *but* was always there.

Clearly, families of both groups had their reservations about the intermarriage of their children. Jewish families, while not actively prohibiting intermarriage, appeared to raise their children with the idea of marrying inside rather than outside the faith. Some families worried about having non-Jewish grandchildren, even though many of the Gentile women in Germany who married Jews converted to Judaism and raised their children as cultural and religious Jews. There were still a few mixed relationships during the early thirties in Sonderburg, but by 1935 intermarriage was legally prohibited by the Nuremberg race laws.

In such smaller communities as Sonderburg, Jews and Gentiles maintained their ethnic distinctiveness despite the many areas where they had common interests and ties. Ethnic relations can best be described in terms of a harmonious accommodation each made to the other's presence—a matter that will be dealt with more fully in Chapter 7. Under such conditions of accommodation, the lines of demarcation were quite clearly drawn.[4] There was a common set of understandings to which both groups subscribed. As Frederick Barth points out, "Stable inter-ethnic relations presuppose a structuring of interaction; a set of prescriptions governing situations of contact, and allowing for articulation in some sectors or domains of activity, and a set of proscriptions on social situations preventing inter-ethnic interaction in other sectors, and thus insulating parts of the cultures from confrontation and modification."[5] Thus, two groups in contact structure or define their interaction. There are rules that allow for interaction and rules that prevent interaction. The latter are particularly important because they prevent one or the other group from losing its cultural identity. Intermarriage was one of the main proscriptions on interethnic contact, and there were few deviations from this rule in Sonderburg. Friendships and dating relationships allowed a certain degree of articulation, for such relationships were part of the larger accommodative interaction between the two groups, as were residential, business, and employment contacts. Intermarriage would have transgressed the commonly accepted ways in which ethnic distinctiveness could not be surrendered. Intermarriage on a larger scale would have led to the dissolution of Jewish culture.

In spite of the large amount of accommodation existing between Jews and Gentiles, full integration or assimilation could not take place because of exclusionist policies in the social arena. That there was also some degree of anti-Semitism is suggested by the fact that at least some people were openly anti-Semitic well before Hitler's time; so no doubt some degree of anti-Semitism was responsible for the lack of intermarriage between the two groups. Of the many close friendships formed between schoolchildren of both groups, few brought about close friendships between the parents. John Miller and his sister had many more Gentile friends than their parents, but the elder Millers' closest friends were the Gentile factory owner and his Jewish wife. Mr. Abraham noted that he had many Gentile acquaintances: "I knew a lot of people, but real friends, no, they were what you call here [in the United States] 'acquaintances.'" The Jews, he notes, "stuck together." His wife recalls that in her home town "the Jewish people lived very nicely together. Gentiles and Jews were friendly to each other, but not friends; the same happened in Sonderburg. People were friendly, they said 'hello' on the street and talked together, but that is not friendship." She remembers working in a Jewish-owned store in Sonderburg with several Gentile girls and "we were very friendly together but only in the store." In my own family, grandparents' friends were other Jews, although they were on friendly terms with many Gentiles. Minna and her parents are an interesting exception. Both she and her parents had more Gentile than Jewish friends, but in her parents' case this had to do with the close ties her father had established as a result of his cultural talents and interests. On the whole, few Jewish adults had true friendships with Gentiles.

Jewish and Gentile respondents describe life in Sonderburg in pre-Hitlerian times as close to ideal—"a small piece of paradise," as one elderly Jew expresses it. Yet this same person (and, of course, others too) depicts clearly the anti-Semitism among some elements in this small community. Was Sonderburg society not marred by such recurrent anti-Semitism earlier in the century? It appears that, as far as the Jews were concerned, they were comfortable, they enjoyed a degree of prosperity and respect from most, if not all, of their neighbors, and they lived in a physically beautiful part of the country. Above all, they considered themselves to be German and they believed in and lived by the same values as did other Germans. Isolated acts of anti-Semitism were apparently not sufficient to disturb their comfort and their satisfaction with life. Their satisfaction was, however, brutally disturbed in the early thirties and they were forced to make major changes in their lives. How did these Jews, who had lived in Germany for generations, react to the growth of Nazism and its subsequent persecution of their people?

Group of children, including the author (front row, center, holding schoolbag), with their teacher, Herr Mannes, at an underground school.

4

JEWISH REACTIONS TO NAZI VICTIMIZATION

Introduction: The Context

"The Nationalist Socialist accession to power sent tremors throughout the Jewish population from right to left."[1] Some responded with suicide, flight, and despair, but others strengthened their will to remain and fight for their rights as German citizens. Dawidowicz writes that "within the Jewish community, every group replied to National Socialism with resounding affirmation of the right of Jews to be German, to live in and love Germany. *Daseinrecht*, the right to maintain a Jewish presence in Germany, was construed as a legal right, a moral necessity and a religous imperative by all Jewish organizations." Nevertheless, in 1933 and 1934 some 37,000 Jews, mostly recent immigrants from Eastern Europe, fled Germany, primarily to other countries in Europe, and many returned to their native Poland and Czechoslovakia, even though Jewish leaders and rabbis consistently appealed to the population to remain and fight for its rights. A leading Jewish newspaper editorialized in 1933 that "Germany will remain Germany and no one can rob us of our homeland and of our fatherland." A prominent leader noted that "it is our aim to preserve within Germany, a German-Jewish community, unbroken financially, physically and spiritually."[2] The newspaper of the Zentralverein, the largest and most influential of the Jewish organizations, wrote in 1934 that "We cannot abandon the ideal of German civilization and spirit." Similarly, the Society for Jewish Aid noted in 1934 that "Our country can solve the Jewish problem provided that racial discrimination does not lead to racial defamation which would, in our estimation, be unacceptable and unjust in view of our past record."[3]

Martin Buber, the famous philosopher, called for a return to Jewish self-awareness and Jewish values—a restoration of individual and community faith in the totality of the Jewish experience. The respected Rabbi Leo Baeck reiterated that Jewry was a "living, effective subject of history" and "each Jew had to discover himself and thus renew his history." Jews returned to the synagogue en masse and sought comfort in their religious observances. There was an urgent need for strong community organization to fight the perils of Nazism since the Jewish community was religiously, politically, and geographically segmented. After many attempts, the Reichsvertretung der deutschen Juden—Federal Representation of German Jews—came into being eight months after the Nazis came to power.[4] Its objective was to help maintain an economic existence, provide aid for those who wanted to emigrate, and defend Jews against defamation. Later in its existence, relief and welfare aid to Jews who had become impoverished were also included. In addition, it helped to provide education for children who had been ousted from the school system after the promulgation in 1933 of the Law Against the Overcrowding of German Schools. It also created retraining programs in the manual trades for civil servants, professionals and business people who had lost their jobs.

From 1933 to 1935, the time of the Nuremberg race laws, the German-Jewish community responded to Nazism by making strong efforts to maintain itself in Germany. From 1935 onward, as increasing surveillance and oppression of the Jews took place, the strong will exercised by the leaders and reflected in the efforts of the population declined. By 1938, the most outspoken defender of *Dasein*—the right to be—Heinrich Stahl, president of the Berlin Jewish Community, said, " 'To those among our youth who have not yet decided to emigrate, I say, there is no future for Jews in this country.' "[5]

By this time, the Nazis were entering into the final phase of their program to oppress Jews since earlier measures had not entirely succeeded in getting all Jews out of Germany. Toward the end of 1937, an article in an SS magazine discussed the "inconsistency between the social status and the economic status of Jews in the Reich." It noted that, although Jews were excluded from almost all areas of institutional life, including intermarriage with non-Jews, they still wielded power in industry and commerce; the author argued that "today we no longer need Jewish business."[6] The government urged that all remaining businesses be sold to non-Jews to exclude Jews from the economic sector entirely.

The effects of these measures on the Jewish occupational structure can be seen in the ways in which it changed between 1933 and 1939, as the following table indicates.

TABLE 1

Changes in the Occupational Structure, 1933 and 1939[7]

Occupation	% of Jews employed, 1933	% of Jews employed, 1939
Agriculture/forestry	1.7	8.9
Industry/crafts	23.1	33.8
Commerce and communication	61.3	18.9
Public and private service	12.5	25.3
Domestic service	1.4	13.1

Thus the commercial sector showed a drop of 42.4 percent whereas agriculture, forestry and domestic service showed an increase of 18.9 percent. The percentages of self-employed or independents dropped from 46.8 percent to 15.7 percent, a net loss of 31.1 percent. Manual laborers increased by nearly 48 percent. A substantial portion of those who had been independent or white collar workers became manual workers.[8]

In Sonderburg, the majority of the independent shopkeepers closed down by 1935–36, and those that did not immediately emigrate remained unemployed. There were few participants in the labor force in this small community. One of my respondents, Albert, said that after being fired from his job in another city in 1933, he worked intermittently prior to his emigration at "whatever jobs I could get." Three younger people had been working for the Millers and remained there until the factory was sold in 1938. Minna had worked at Kahn's department store but she transferred to the Millers, who replaced her at Kahn's with one of their Gentile workers. Alice continued at whatever hairdressing jobs were available among the remaining Jewish women, but by the mid-1930s, few women were able to use her services.

In 1938 remaining Jewish institutions, such as the Gemeinde, had their corporate status revoked. In the same year, the annexation of Austria took place, accompanied by the horrendous persecution of the large Jewish community in Vienna. Because the Austrian Nazis were busily seizing Jewish property, new decrees were enacted in 1938 legitimizing the disposal of Jewish properties "according to the needs of the German economy."[9] Large numbers of Jews were rounded up and detained in concentration camps, and in the communities of Munich, Nuremberg, and Dortmund, synagogues were completely disrupted and their property taken over by the Nazis.

By now the flow of emigration had increased, but the major difficulty was in finding countries that would accept Jews. The Evian conference was initiated by President Roosevelt in 1938 to confront the problems of German and Austrian Jews in response to Hitler's invasion of Austria, which raised a storm of protest among liberals in the United States. Thirty-three nations were invited to the conference to discuss solutions to the crisis. But the American delegates had no intention of providing further aid to Jews, since all they announced at the conference was that the United States emigration quota for German and Austrian Jews would be adhered to. (In earlier years, the quota had not been fully met.) Germany allowed Jewish spokesmen to attend the conference, and, in addition, there were representatives of nearly forty Jewish organizations from many parts of the world. All of these groups were heard in one afternoon. The World Jewish Congress, representing seven million Jews, was allowed five minutes, whereas the groups from Germany were not heard at all. They were asked instead to submit a written brief for inclusion in the minutes. The conference concluded with a resolution that the nations of the world "were not willing to undertake any obligations towards financing involuntary immigration."[10] A recent book notes that "Evian had clearly shown that none wanted Jews."[11]

In Germany, Nazi leaders now had sufficient evidence to show that no country would intercede on behalf of the Jews. A leading newspaper announced in large headline type: "JEWS FOR SALE— WHO WANTS THEM? NO ONE." Another stated: "We note that sympathy is shown to the Jews so long as it encourages agitation against Germany, but no country is prepared to remove central Europe's cultural defects by accepting a few thousand Jews. The conference has therefore vindicated the German policy towards the Jews."[12]

Until this time, the oppression of Jews had been undertaken by representatives of the legal and judicial system. However, the outrage committed against Jewish homes, businesses, synagogues and cemeteries during the night of November 9, 1938, was claimed to have been the work of the German population, a "spontaneous wave of righteous indignation throughout Germany, as a result of the cowardly Jewish murder of Third Secretary von Rath in the German Embassy at Paris."[13] In fact, Kristallnacht was the carefully orchestrated work of the SA and the SS, and its illegality outraged the majority of the German population. The horrors of this nationwide pogrom against the Jews and the beginnings of their deportation to concentration (and later death) camps destroyed what was left of the Jewish community in Germany.

Reactions to Nazism in Sonderburg

In Sonderburg, as elsewhere, Jewish reaction to Nazism varied according to age group. People in their twenties and thirties more readily believed the threat to Jews and made preparations to leave the country as soon as possible. Their parents, having spent many more years in Sonderburg and being established in their trades and professions, could scarcely believe that the Jews would be destroyed. Many older people were firmly convinced that it would all blow over after a while and that the Nazi regime would disintegrate because it was such an abberration in an otherwise orderly history. As yet, no one believed that Hitler would start a war of such major proportions or that he would embark on systematic genocide against the Jews. Most still trusted that in the next election—although after 1933 none was proposed—the German people who were good and decent would vote the regime out of office. As a respondent, Martha, declared, pounding her fist on the table for emphasis, "I would never have believed that this would have happened, never, never, never!" Still, despite their optimistic view, older people urged their children to leave, and by 1934 several younger members of families had gone. By 1936 many more had emigrated, primarily to the United States, some via England, Holland and France.

Until 1939 and the beginning of the Final Solution, the Nazi regime attempted through legal enactments and harassment to force the Jews out of Germany. Although at the official level emigration was encouraged, the process involved was long, arduous, and costly. It became even more difficult during the later years. Unfortunately, in 1938 and 1939, after both Kristallnacht and the Evian conference, when large numbers of Jews finally attempted to emigrate to the United States, the Americans gave out quota numbers and people had to wait until their numbers came up. Even today, some remember their quota numbers. One woman recalled that hers was exactly 11000, and another remembered hers to be 19480. Because of the large numbers of people involved, some numbers would not have become due until 1940, or even well into the war. Even Jews waiting to go to England, France or Holland required sponsorship to enter these countries, and only those lucky enough to have contacts there were able to make such arrangements. Minna, whose American quota number would have come due in 1940, described how she and her parents left Germany for England in April and May 1939:

> But I didn't go to America right away. After the house was sold and the furniture was sent, I went to England and five weeks later, I brought my parents to England. When I left them, I said "I will bring you over." My father replied, "You will never see us again." I said, "I will bring you over, I give you my word and even before I take a job (I was supposed to be a domestic worker), I will do everything to bring you over." I got over on account of my cousin who married an Englishman, but he couldn't help me, he sent me to the Society of Friends. I told him [the man at the Society] that we had our ship tickets already to go to America and my brother is in America already and we had a sponsor there. We would take care of my parents if anybody would help me in bringing them to England, not financially, only as a sponsor. While I talked to him, I will never forget it, he said to me—he was a Mr. Howard—"Wait a minute," and he spoke to a lady. When he came back, he said, "That lady who was just leaving will take the sponsorship of your parents." So I asked him to give me that address of the lady, I only wanted to thank her, and he said, "No thanks are necessary, we do it for humanity's sake."

Shortly afterward Minna received a letter from Mr. Howard informing her that her parents could come to England and all they had to do was get the necessary papers from the English consulate. Her father was confused and desperate by this time; "instead of calling the Consulate, in Frankfurt, he went there and they told him they didn't have papers for him. He sent me a cable saying, 'there are no papers and I'm sure we won't be able to come.' So I sent a cable to the British embassy in Berlin and five days later I was told the papers had been sent to Frankfurt. I sent my father a cable 'Go to Frankfurt again, the papers are there,' and they came on the 22nd of May, 1939."

Despite all these complications, their trip was expedited by the generosity of the Quakers; but their relief at arriving in England was marred by the father's internment: "My father was interned in England, this came after Dunkirk and they took the men regardless of age because they were afraid that a few Nazis were smuggled in. It could have happened, you know. Just give them Jewish names and send them over." Minna's father was eventually released and shortly thereafter the family emigrated to the United States.[14]

Mr. Martin remembers that after Kristallnacht he left his home and went to Mainz to his sister. From that point on,

> all that I worked on was to try to get out of this country. I would have left earlier but my mother didn't want to go, she was born here, her husband had died here. But after Kristallnacht, even she was convinced, and at this time there was such a flood of people trying to get out and go to America that they were given out numbers. Our number was 12345. We had to wait until we were called. My sister was there already, and she had to borrow $1,000 to send us money for our tickets. We came with just the clothes on our backs even though we were not poor—we were middle-class. We went to Frankfurt, then we were told we had to go to Berlin. In Berlin the Jewish organization tried to get us a passage but first we had to go to Vienna. Finally, we left by boat from Spain and arrived in New York in 1939.

For others the process of leaving was just as harrowing. One family went to Holland and from there to England and then to the United States. In another case, a family had secured its affidavit and quota number to the United States but had to wait for space on a boat. The next such boat was leaving from France, and an entry permit for France was difficult to secure and required more time, effort, and particularly bribe money because France, along with other European countries, had already closed its borders to Jews. Bribing officialdom was a common experience for many persons attempting to expedite their departure and, in a few instances, it involved the bribing of Jewish officials who worked for Jewish self-help organizations.

The need for money during this period was intense, and those who had some savings were fortunate. One man relates that he spent more money during that year than in three years of ordinary living. Minna and her parents managed to sell their house in Sonderburg and thus had enough money for emigration. Since she had also worked for many years in the Kahn department store, she had some savings of her own. Younger people used money donated by their parents, who were for the moment staying behind. Family resources were pooled in order to allow younger members to emigrate. Once they had the necessary quota number and the affidavit from an American relation, they had to arrange boat passage, usually from France, Holland, Spain, or via Holland to England and then to New York. Several families managed to enter England and awaited their affidavits there. In at least two cases from this community (Minna's story was described earlier), the adult male members of the family were imprisoned by British authorities, who feared that they might be spying for Germany. Martha, then a girl of eighteen, describes the relief that she felt upon entering England.

> We finally arrived on English soil after waiting for eight months for our exit quota, and while we were waiting to clear customs and immigration, my mother and I cried with relief. We cleared our baggage and went to immigration. Suddenly, the officer told my father he had to go into another room. He returned later and told my mother and me that father would be put into prison on suspicion of spying. He was kept there for four months—I visited every week and tried to keep his spirits up. Finally, our affidavit arrived, and he was released and sent straight from the jail with a guard who went with him right to the boat.

In my own family, my father was arrrested the morning after Kristallnacht and sent to Dachau. My mother and I were left behind with no resources since the family had long since used up its small savings in the course of day-to-day living. Fortunately, as noted in the Introduction, we were given a sum of money by a non-Jewish brother-in-law. The money sustained us during these times and also allowed my mother to bribe various officials in order to secure my father's release. She was told exactly how to secure his release by a friendly magistrate, who had known the family and was eager to see it leave the country. The family needed an entrance permit into France, and she relates how she obtained it:

> I traveled to the French consulate in Stuttgart. The secretary there told me no more entrance permits were being issued. I didn't know what to do and just hung around the office. At 5:00 o'clock, I saw

a tall, distinguished-looking man come out of the office and I thought he must be the consul. I rushed up to him and explained our desperate situation and that we needed a permit and that my husband would not be released from Dachau without it. He looked at me and said, "Meet me at the hotel tomorrow evening for dinner." I was ready to do anything. I searched for my best dress, ironed it and bought some new makeup. I even washed and styled my hair. If he wanted to go to bed with me, I would do it. I would have done anything for that piece of paper. We met, he ordered wine and a very expensive meal—the best I had had in a year—we talked about everything under the sun except the situation and politics. He paid the bill and I thought, "here it comes," he will now suggest we go to a room upstairs. As we reached the door, he stopped, reached into his breast pocket and gave me the permit and said, "You are a courageous woman, good luck to you and your family." A week later my husband returned from Dachau by train, looking thin and haggard and so on; three days later, we got on a train to France, and when I saw the French Tricolor in front of me, I became hysterical.

For many others the process of leaving Germany was just as arduous. People would be sent from one administrative office to another, often on a flimsy pretext, and since these offices were located in different cities, this meant a good deal of traveling and considerable expense. Final papers, passports, bank clearance, and internal revenue clearance were all necessary for departure. Most middle-class emigrés, no longer employed, had to use their small savings, borrowing money and selling off possessions as they roamed from city to city. Mr. Martin had to bribe a Jewish lawyer who secured for him a boat passage from Spain. He recalls, "I had to bribe the lawyer for the Jewish organization in Berlin 500 marks [a considerable sum in those days] so that they would put me on a train—all because everybody wanted to go at the same time. When we went to Berlin, we slept on the floor of the Jewish organization's office and they told me that the 500 marks was for that." Mr. Martin and his mother arrived in the United States with only the clothes on their backs. Others were more fortunate. Despite the many difficulties encountered in the emigration process, a substantial number of people were able to take their possessions with them even as late as 1938–40. The regime dictated that Jews had to declare their money and valuables, particularly gold and silver, and such items could not be removed from the country. Furniture, household items, and clothing could be taken. The younger members of the Miller family took many trunks with them, as did most people who left in the mid-1930s. Even later, as much as could be packed and transported was taken along. My parents, and my aunt and uncle were able to pack, between them, a very large set of china. In some cases, valuables were smuggled out, sometimes with the complicity of a kindly customs official. John recalled that he knew a Gentile who would create false heels in shoes and boots in which small valuables could be hidden. Minna related how she was able to smuggle out a set of sterling silver cutlery:

> When I made out the list of what we had, and they said to mark down everything, I said I had a silver set for eighteen people. There was an official from the tax office in Kreuzen who heard that they were taking gold and silver from the Jews. He was in Sonderburg visiting friends and he called to tell me something. We met and we were standing in front of a store window pretending to look in. He said, "Minna, I know you want to go away and I'm glad you do, but did you by any chance mark down any silver on your documents for the government?" I said, "Yes, I have marked down a cutlery set for eighteen people." So he said, "Go out and buy plated silver. They will come in and inspect and you show them those," which I did. So, when they came, they said, "You marked down sterling silver." I said, "Isn't that sterling silver?" "No, it's only plated." "Well, that's all I have," I said and they left. When we packed, I put the real silver between my clothes. When I came to customs, I gave the man the big package and said, "Help me, give it to them [the transporters]," so he helped me smuggle out the silver without knowing it.

She realized that she was taking a big risk, but her father went even further:

> My father took his stamp collection with him which he took out stamp by stamp and put them on the back of a mirror. The mirror was too heavy for us so I said to the customs man, "That mirror is too heavy, will you take it [to the loaders]?" He took it and said "My goodness, it is heavy, it's a good thing that I'm here." So both the silver and the stamps got out with his help. But if his man from Kreuzen wouldn't have told me to do this—you see—there was always somebody who had a way.

Jews could only take a very small amount of money, so many attempted, even at great risk, to pack and, if need be, smuggle whatever they had. Several people, as in Minna's case, claimed that they had been helped by German civil servants in negotiating their emigration. In my own case, my mother was advised by a magistrate, a former friend of the family, in how to secure the release of my father from Dachau. His advice included exactly who to bribe and how much.

These cases illustrate the difficulty Jews had in leaving Germany during the late thirties. Earlier, of course, the process was somewhat easier but all emigrants had to tangle with the bureaucracy in order to get passports, financial and tax clearance, and other documents in Germany, as well as sponsorship documents and visas to get into other parts of Europe, the United States, and elsewhere. Many people could have been spared such hardships had they emigrated earlier But the need for foreign sponsorship, combined with the reluctance on the part of some Jews to leave Germany, had stood in the way. By 1938–39, the complicity of foreign countries in denying them entrance was to lead to the loss of many lives.

Emigration in Sonderburg (and Germany)

There were 150 Jews in Sonderburg before 1933. As will be seen from the table below, about half managed to emigrate.

TABLE 2

What happened to the Sonderburg Jews

Died during 1930s or before of natural causes	32
Emigrated to the United States directly from Sonderburg	38
Emigrated to the United States via other German cities	8
Emigrated to England	13
(7 went to the United States later)	
Emigrated to France	10
(1 went to the United States; 1 returned to Germany)	
Emigrated to Israel	4
Emigrated to other countries—Holland, Canada	3
Went to other cities in Germany, whereabouts unknown thereafter	21
Changed religion and moved	2
Deported from Sonderburg	12
Deported from other cities	7
	150

Thus, over 50 percent, seventy-six in number, managed to emigrate to other countries. Of the twenty-one persons who left Sonderburg for other cities in Germany, many, if not all, were probably deported to death camps so that we can assume that between thirty and forty of the Sonderburg Jews (or approximately 23 percent of the population) lost their lives in death camps. This figure is probably somewhat lower than the national average since probably close to 40 percent of the German Jews lost their lives in death camps. More people from Sonderburg than in the country as a whole were able to emigrate.

The Jews of Sonderburg were following a national trend as emigration statistics from these years indicate. Table 3 displays the figures.

TABLE 3

Jewish population figures: 1933, 1939, 1944[15]

Year	Jews of faith*	Jews of birth	Persons with 2 Jewish grandparents**	Persons with 1 Jewish grandparent	Total
1933	499,682	40,000			539,682
1939	213,930	19,716	52,005	32,669	318,320
1945				(hidden)	14,574
				(survived camps)	5,000

* The census distinguished between Jews who subscribed to their faith and Jews who were born into Jewish families but who no longer subscribed to Judaism or who had converted to Christianity.
** The Nuremberg Laws of 1935 classified as Jews those who had one or two Jewish grandparents.

These figures reveal that the population of about 540,000 in 1933 was decreased by 520,000, or over 96 percent, by 1945. This decrease was caused by natural deaths (68,000), deportation to camps (135,000) and emigration (317,000); of those emigrating, about 30,000 went to other parts of occupied Europe, where a high proportion were killed in camps. Approximately 20,000 Jews either survived the camps or were successfully hidden during the war.

The majority of Jews fleeing Germany tried to get into the United States. Figures gathered by H. Strauss are quite revealing in showing that until 1939 the American quota established for Germany was consistently undersubscribed. The United States in 1925 had established a quota system of immigration which allowed for 25,000 Germans, plus an additional 2,000 from Austria. The following table gives the figures:

TABLE 4

Emigration to the United States

Year	1933	1934	1935	1936	1937	1938	1939	1940
Numbers	1,450	3,740	5,530	6,650	11,520	17,870	27,370	26,080
Percent	5.5	13.7	20.2	24.3	42.1	65.3	100	95.3
Percentage of Germans as percent of total immigrants	6.2	12.6	15.8	18.3	23	26.3	33	36.8

Thus, it was not until 1939 that the quota was fully subscribed, and only twice during this period was the German Jewish emigration one-third or more of the total emigration to the United States, in the years 1939 and 1940. Strauss attributes the low figures to the fact that, under American law, proof of support was necessary and many Jews had difficulty in finding sponsors to sign their affidavits.[16] Those who had family members already in the United States could claim sponsorship more easily but many were not so fortunate.

As in Sonderburg, the height of emigration was reached in 1938, when 40,000 Jews emigrated, and in the following year, when 78,000 Jews left Germany. The Sonderburg figures differ only in that somewhat more than three-fifths of the Jewish population there was able to emigrate and fewer than the national average lost their lives in camps. The process of emigration, while long and arduous and fraught with tension and difficulties, was nevertheless eased for the people in Sonderburg because many of them had established relatives in the United States who could sponsor them. Otherwise entry would have been impossible. Luckily, many Sonderburgers had emigrated to the United States earlier in the century. In one family, a great-aunt had left in 1911, at the age of seventeen. She married an American and raised American-born children, who were able to act as sponsors for her two brothers and a sister. The Martin family was sponsored by an uncle who had emigrated in 1919. All the members of the large Miller family were also sponsored by an uncle who had been in the United States for many years. In a few cases, family members who had emigrated early in the thirties, though not yet American citizens, nevertheless sent financial help to their kin and particularly the money for passage and related expenses. Families without American relatives had the greatest difficulty in leaving Germany, and those that managed to do so went to England and Holland. Thus the American connection was a vital link in the emigration process. Ironically enough, there were two instances in two separate Sonderburg families where emigration to the United States had taken place many years before this period, but the emigrés decided to return to Germany. Information available for one family revealed that the man had had some severe business reverses in 1920, was still in his late twenties, and unmarried, although engaged. Since his fiancée's sister had already established herself in New York, he paid a visit to see if he should settle there as well. He spent several months in America, decided that he did not really like the country, preferring the old-world culture of Germany, and so returned. He opened another business, married, raised a family of four children, and eventually perished in Theresianstadt, a concentration camp in Czechoslovakia.

Thus, despite the earlier valiant efforts to sustain their existence in Germany, the primary response of German Jewry to their increasing victimization was to leave as soon as circumstances permitted. In Sonderburg the dozen people who were left behind were all older people who had wanted their children to have the first chance at emigration. My own grandparents, who had prepared to emigrate as soon as my parents were safely established in the United States, gave up their American quota number to the teen-age children of a distant cousin. Apparently, the cousin visited them in desperation because she was by then unable to secure a number. The old couple decided that they had lived their lives and wanted to give the young teen-agers a chance in a new country and so gave their number to them. Despite many efforts by my grandparents to begin the emigration process again for themselves, they did not succeed and were deported in 1942.

Life in Sonderburg During the Thirties

What was life like for the Jews in Sonderburg during the 1930s? Although many of them were in the process of emigrating, they had, nevertheless, to live on a day-to-day basis in their town. One obvious result of their victimization was that, starting early in 1933, they were increasingly isolated from all facets of Sonderburg life. (The breakdown of relations with Gentile associates and friends is described in detail in the next chapter). Curiously enough, however, their social life was not completely curtailed since they could always go to the larger towns and cities, where they were not known as Jews. This was, of course, before 1939, when all Jews were forced to wear the yellow arm band in order to clearly identify them as Jews.

Traditionally, the social life of both Sonderburg Jews and Gentiles, especially those of middle and upper class status, had always included visits and trips to the neighboring larger towns and cities. Many went on special shopping expeditions or to visit friends and relatives who lived out of the town. Well-to-do Jews and Gentiles regularly went to Kreuzen or even Frankfurt to see movies, or to attend the theater, concerts, and operas. They also went abroad on holidays—to France and Switzerland and elsewhere. Despite Sonderburg's small size, the town had always been well served by the railway system, so that transportation even in earlier times presented little difficulty. These patterns continued throughout the thirties. While socializing within Sonderburg became impossible, visits and trips to other cities continued. Small groups of younger Jews still enjoyed excursions into the countryside, as they had in earlier times. I have several photos of my father and other younger Jews in Sonderburg taken while they were enjoying boat trips on the river or picnics in the countryside even as late as 1936–37. Some still went to Frankfurt to see movies and dine at restaurants. One young man spent considerable amounts of time in Frankfurt, where he had gone to school and had many Jewish and half-Jewish friends. Since he had, of necessity, lost his Gentile friends in Sonderburg, he spent much of his leisure visiting former school friends in Frankfurt. Another man, who had learned to play tennis while at school abroad, continued playing regularly but only within Jewish networks in other cities. A few Jews even attended Nazi party rallies held in other towns and cities in order to gather information. For example, Albert and two Jewish friends traveled to Oberstadt, some thirty kilometers away, in the company of Herr Tiller and a few other Gentiles late in 1934. The Jews were not recognized as Jews, and no one in the small group, Jew or Gentile, gave the "Heil Hitler" salute.

In his recent autobiography, Rabbi Gunther Plaut makes clear how the pattern of Jewish life changed. His words apply equally well to the experience of Jews in Sonderburg:

> I was emotionally half asleep, lulled into a sense of false security by the gradualness of much of the Nazis' official antisemitic program. Our ghetto was social and intellectual, not physical. We simply shifted our focus away from the Germany in which we had lived to an exclusively Jewish ambience; in theatre, in music and

in sports. . . . I played soccer with Hakoah's first team, which met other Jewish formations from different cities and even from Vienna; and I played tennis at Bar Kochba. . . . Instead of competing with Germans, we now played against Jews, but otherwise, the tournaments were like any others; the enthusiasm, the desire to win, were no different. Just before I began my written tests I won the German-Jewish championship in tennis singles. . . . We entered tournaments in various German cities as if the Nazis didn't exist. We were quartered with the finest Jewish families and had a wonderful time. It was a new make-believe world, we were half dead but thought we were alive, we believed that it would all blow over in time.[17]

Thus, starting in 1933, most Sonderburg Jews conducted their social life outside of Sonderburg. Within the town, Jewish people would still visit each other's homes, but encounters outside of the privacy of the home were not encouraged. People would greet each other on the street or in other public places but they would quickly part because, as Mr. Abraham noted, "if two or three Jews stood on a street corner, then groups of SA men would come up at any time to harass them or beat them up." When people did visit each other, the content of their conversation almost always revolved around questions of strategy. As Martha recalled, "We were always talking about who was leaving, where were they going and what can we do?" One of the problems, aside from emigration, was where and how to dispose of property so that one had cash in hand to purchase or arrange the purchase of basic necessities such as food, and money for bribes and for traveling to and from various administrative centers. Jews who were emigrating also had to arrange the sale of their businesses and homes. Even though the law allowed Jewish businesses to operate until the late thirties, in practice, small-business men and retailers began selling off and closing down much earlier.[18] In Sonderburg, only the Miller factory remained in Jewish hands until the end of 1938. By the mid-thirties, most merchants had closed their shops, since their volume of trade, reduced to only Jewish customers, was no longer sufficient to keep them in business. Just prior to emigrating, Jews also sold their homes.

These transactions were, in the main, done locally. The rental of the Kahn department store to a merchant in a nearby town was accomplished when it became known that Kahn and his brother-in-law were eager to emigrate to France. One of their employees became manager of the store, and he later purchased it from Kahn, who returned after the war to settle his business. As related in Chapter

1, the Miller factory was almost sold in 1936 to a large company for somewhere near its market value, but Mr. Miller changed his mind; two years later he sold the factory to the same company for substantially less money. Dr. Ritter, its director, was still doing business, traveling abroad to visit customers and take orders, until a few weeks before his departure to the United States in 1939. The Mandels sold their dry goods store to a neighbor who had always been interested in becoming a retail shopkeeper. Again, the price was far below its actual value. Local Gentiles, in fact, were quick to seize the opportunity when they realized that they could purchase some of the best business and residential properties in Sonderburg at a fraction of their actual value. Minna's father, taking one example, sold the family home to one of his former school friends "who heard we were leaving. He came over one night and said he wanted to buy it. The house was valued at 21,000 marks, but he told father that since it was a Jewish house, he had to pay only 13,000 marks for it." In a few cases, Jews simply left their homes because their visas and other documents became effective before they could sell their property. And, of course, the homes of several old Jews who were deported eventually became the property of the Reichsvereinigung (the Jewish organization by then under Gestapo control) and were sold after the war. One exception was old Mr. Miller's home, which had been willed to his Gentile housekeeper. Herr Hammer purchased my grandparents' house in the early 1950s. His family had lived next door, where his father owned a small shop. Herr Hammer told me that, had his father known that the Jews were going to be deported and that the Ostermans would be part of that deportation, he "would have made them a generous offer even then." As it was, his son finally bought the house from my family, through a lawyer in Germany, when he wanted to expand his business.

So a considerable amount of time and effort was expended during the 1930s in the various financial transactions involving the sale of properties. However, insofar as they could, people remained at work. Shopkeepers worked in their stores until the mid-thirties, when most closed down. The senior Miller, his son-in-law, and others involved in the Miller business also continued working. There were very few Jewish people in the labor force, but those who were tried to keep their jobs as long as possible. For a few, such as Albert, who worked in a Gentile firm in another city, loss of employment came early, but four young Jews employed by the Millers continued to work through 1938.

It might be expected that religious observances were more actively pursued during this period, as they were elsewhere in Germany. Such was not the case in Sonderburg, however. People who went to the synagogue on the Sabbath and on the holidays continued to do so, but there was no particular increase in synagogue activities. Synagogue services and attendance, of course, stopped completely after Kristallnacht, when the building was burned and partially demolished.

By 1939 only twelve Jews were left in Sonderburg and they were finally deported in 1942. What was life like for these dozen stranded old people whose every hope for exit was thwarted and who were left behind to die? On the surface, they had resigned themselves to the inevitability of their fate. Most stayed in their homes, fearing the hostility they would encounter on the street. They were living in one or two rooms in their homes since they had been forced to rent the remaining space to German families. Their small quarters were poorly furnished since so many of their possessions had been demolished during Kristallnacht. They could no longer shop in the stores, though friendly neighbors brought them food secretly at night. Irmgard, a Gentile woman then seventeen years old and the daughter of a carpenter, lived directly across the street from a Jewish family of two adults, plus a widower who was forced to move in with them since his home had been totally demolished. She recalls, "We were fairly well off for food even in the early forties because my mother came from a farm family and we have good connections to the land. We got fresh vegetables, potatoes and cereals, and sometimes fresh meat from the farmers. Every morning my mother put aside a portion and said it was for them. Late that night, she would rush across the street and give it to them. They never went out much." In those last years, the twelve Jews were divided among five homes (one woman had been in a clinic for a mental disorder but was being boarded with an old couple who cared for her). All five homes were regularly visited late at night by friendly neighbors who brought food and some of whom would stay awhile, knowing how isolated the Jews were. Irmgard notes that her mother would often stay with the Jewish neighbors "just for a half-hour to chat with them. They were so alone."

The best evidence of the isolation comes from the letters Jews wrote to their families in the United States. I was fortunate to receive a number of letters kept by the Miller family and sent to them by their great-uncle, who had chosen to remain behind, thinking himself too old to start life anew in another country. His incredible loneliness and isolation is frequently recorded. As a footnote to the times, Mr. Miller had to give his name as Henning "Israel" Miller on his return address, for all Jews since 1938 were ordered by law to assume the name of either Israel or Sarah to indicate their Jewishness. These passages come from the letters he wrote in 1940:

> Your letter took 8 weeks to reach me—it had to pass English and German censors. I am overjoyed to hear anything from you and that everything goes well for you. You can be proud of all your accomplishments in so short a time. I wish I could see your business. Sometimes I am homesick for you all since I was with you for most of your lives. I hope I will soon be called by the big army upstairs. From Purim, Passover, nothing happens here—one day is like another. From here there is nothing new. The weather has turned nice. . . .

> You are living as free persons, for me, a change in older years is difficult. My legs are going and the eyes are getting weaker so I can't read at nights. Sometimes I play cards with Marie to kill the time. I didn't observe the Holidays. . . . Your birthdays are celebrated among your family and I too would wish to be there but that remains a fond hope. Here there is not much to report. The Landau family now lives in the Jewish Community House in Neuegasse. The Wolf family is there too. Everyone has a room and a kitchen and upstairs lives the family Heymann.

> Here there is one day like the next. Nothing changes. I hope this existence will end soon. Here 4 people died . . . [names four Gentile names]. Mrs. Diego told Marie that on April 20, she goes to Genoa to go to the U.S.A. [This is a Gentile family.] I sold shares for 7,000 marks and I hope this is the last because I hope not to live too much longer.

> In the newspaper I read that it is hot there. Here it is very cool. I am well but weary of life, I am now old enough. Albert and Loeb were here [from Köln] for a visit and I had a change of routine. He goes from here to Wiesbaden but he has no job. Luis had an appendicitis operation. Emil Kahn recently lost his wife [these are all Gentiles]. The burial will be in Kreuzen but I will not go, I'm no longer fond of traveling.

> I am still fairly satisfied but no one comes to me and I don't go out. Marie is my only company. But yesterday Mr. Gottschalk from Kirk passed through and stopped in. We are waiting for fresh vegetables after the winter. No spinach yet but now is asparagus time. The potatoes are particularly good this year. We still get enough to eat.

Later, in 1941, Mr. Miller wrote:

I thank you for your good wishes. I hope this is my last birthday.
Marie sometimes buys wine from Hartmans winery but it was wet
and the wine is not good this year.

The last letter the family received, in August 1941, contains these
words:

We enjoy your letters—they are our only change, the only new
thing in our lives. Many people still ask after you and today Marie
spoke to Frau Lentner who hopes you are doing well.

From the mundane nature of these letters, it is quite obvious
that Mr. Miller knew the letters were opened and so he never described the hardships of life under the regime. Nor did he relate any
political or current events occurring in Germany, though he was
still aware of them since he avidly read the newspapers. He wrote
only of routine matters, of his health, and of the kinds of food that
his household could still buy. He was particularly well off, probably
in a better position than any of the other remaining Jews since he
had money and was in the care of his Gentile housekeeper, who
remained with him until his deportation. She was able to purchase
food and other items as required without hindrance. He had few
contacts with the remaining Jews, and only in one letter did he
write about his meeting with another Jew, who helped him by typing
a certificate a cousin needed for emigration. The few people he did
report on were mainly Gentiles—with the single exception of two
Jews from Cologne (Köln)—and the information had been relayed
to him by Marie, the housekeeper. What old Mr. Miller did not
mention in his letters were his two attempts at suicide. Some time
before the deportation, he asked his housekeeper to burn documents
and family pictures because he did not want anything of value to
fall into the wrong hands. On one occasion, he went to a doctor and
asked for a shot that would kill him, which the doctor refused. On
another occasion, he went to the river and tried to drown himself
but was picked up by someone and brought back home.

Another series of letters, written by my grandparents to their
sons and daughter in the United States, describes more social contact with the remaining Jewish group. They were then both in their
sixties and, although they gave their quota number to distant relatives, they made almost daily efforts to emigrate. Their letters are

full of details with respect to departure regulations, as this excerpt from their last letter, written in November 1941, illustrates:

> We received your telegram but it was 6 weeks underway. We can't telegraph from here when we want to. I am in touch with the travel organization in Essen about the Cuba visit but we must have the transit visa to Spain and Portugal. But there is no transport from Berlin to Lisbon now. We don't know if we can leave from Lisbon and we don't know about the Cuba visa.

Earlier, in July 1941, my grandfather had written:

> Since we don't know if we can come with the American transport from Lisbon, maybe you should get your money back from them. Walter writes that his visa has not arrived. Arrangements are being made with the self-help organization in Cologne, and if something good comes of it, I will telegraph immediately.

In August 1941 he had sent us this information:

> We sent you our certificates and also some photocopies and the waiting numbers. Maybe that will help from your side. Nothing new about our departure. We heard that those with certificates could still get a visa and come out. Tomorrow we are ordered to Kreuzen to fill out another questionnaire. Everything is still good with us.

Many other parts of these letters set out the administrative trials my grandparents had to endure. It would appear that their time was filled with—ultimately futile—attempts to emigrate to the United States. Their letters also contain mention of other Sonderburg Jews and other members of their family still in Germany with whom they were in frequent contact. In May 1941, they had sent this bit of news to the family: "Mrs. Haas is still in hospital in Frankfurt and the latest word is that she has leukemia, so Dr. Hoenich tells us. 14 days ago we took Mrs. Kahn to the same hospital in Frankfurt and while there visited Mrs. Haas." In another letter, my grandfather noted that Mrs. Mextler was then also in the hospital and that they had recently visited all three of the patients from Sonderburg. The hospital was a Jewish one—the only place where Jews at this time were still being accepted for treatment. In another letter, he mentioned that "Milton Hardt last week received four letters from the U.S. We have heard nothing from you." In still another note, he wrote that he was going to Stuttgart in "behalf of Mrs. Marx in Sonderburg" to see about her possible departure. With respect to the family, these letters refer frequently to his having heard from Eric in Sweden, who, in turn, had heard from his aunt and uncle in Israel; "also the Bochum family writes regularly." In addition, they were in constant touch with Walter, a cousin who was "better informed than we," and in one letter they tell of having just returned from Stattheim, a nearby village, where they visited with grandmother's sister and her Gentile husband, who were still alive and healthy. Although my grandparents wrote nothing about domestic happenings, they frequently noted that "everything is still well with us, we are healthy." Life, in other words, proceeded normally even in the last year. But their sadness is moving when they frequently express the wish to be with their family again. In one letter, my grandmother wrote, "The long wait is terrible, if we were only with you but that will still take a long time," and "I hope we can spend this coming summer with you." The letters are also characterized by a never-yielding hope that emigration would be possible, making my grandparents' eventual deportation to a concentration camp all the more saddening. The letters stopped in November 1941. America's entry into World War II in December 1941 prevented further communication.

My grandparents and the other remaining Jews waited out their last years in solitude, isolated from the community in which they were born and raised. They had led fairly prosperous and comfortable lives in Sonderburg, had established businesses, raised children and lived much the same kind of lives as everyone else in the community. From 1939, however, they were almost prisoners in their homes, their entire lives completely circumscribed by fear and isolation. As Dickinson comments, recounting the life of a Jewish lawyer in a small community called Hochberg, "The Jews were the official pariahs of Hochberg [read, Sonderburg] and Germany and by the early forties, their pariah status was complete."[19]

Despite the fact that his status was that of a pariah, my grandfather in these last years was still forced to become involved in a legal transaction with the Nazi regime. The matter involved the sale of a Jewish synagogue building in the nearby village of Stattheim.[20] The village had had a tiny Jewish community consisting of a handful of families, but by the late 1930s probably no Jews remained there with the exception of my grandmother's sister, who had married a Gentile many years earlier. As the only Jew there and married to a non-Jew, she was apparently protected by her husband

and neighbors and lived undisturbed throughout this period and even during the war. By 1939 my grandfather was one of the few remaining male members of the Sonderburg Jewish community and the only one who had kin ties to Stattheim. Perhaps because of these factors, he had to assume the role of local sales agent for the synagogue property. By this time, many Jewish properties came under the jurisdiction of the Reichsvereinigung, or Federal Union of Jews in Germany, as had this synagogue property. Their representatives urged grandfather to expedite the sale ("I am continually urged by those in Berlin to take care of the matter") because the citizens of Stattheim wished to purchase the property. From about 1938 he was involved in a variety of legal proceedings that included arranging for the assessment of the property, payment of assessment fees, claiming ownership certificates, and other bureaucratic procedures, which involved a considerable amount of time and effort in letter writing and traveling. One document sets a date for assessment and states curtly that the "Jew, Jacob Israel Osterman, is to be notified of the date." The transactions were slow and cumbersome, and led grandfather to write in July 1941 that "I have been working on this matter now for over four years and would like to have it taken care of before my departure." This plaintive appeal elicited a response a few days later from the magistrate's office to the mayor of Sonderburg, which ended with the suggestion that the "purchase be concluded as the Jew, Osterman, would like to bring the matter to a close before his forthcoming emigration."

My grandfather's hoped-for emigration, destined never to take place, was thus recorded in these official transcripts. The sadness of involvement in a legal procedure with representatives of the regime who refer to him contemptuously as the "Jew" or "the Jew Osterman" is overwhelming. The final set of documents for the transaction date from the spring of 1943 and affirm that the property was sold. In April 1943, a letter from the regional office of the Nazi party endorsed the sale and proclaimed officially that the property was legally "desemitized" or "dejewified." The transaction was completed eight months after my grandparents were deported and about four months after my grandfather's death in the concentration camp of Theresianstadt.

For the Jews who emigrated life was beginning anew, whereas for most of those left behind, death in the concentration camps ended their persecution. How did the Gentile population, many of whom had befriended Jews, react to the persecution of their friends?

Gravestones showing the marks of destruction which took place during Kristallnacht.

5

GERMAN REACTIONS TO THE PERSECUTION OF JEWS

Broken Friendships

Frau von Himmel is a slight, frail-looking woman in her eighties. She lives in one of the oldest houses in Sonderburg—dating back to 1784. It is surrounded by a courtyard, which still contains animal stalls although she and her family no longer keep livestock. When I interviewed her, she was wearing an old printed cotton dress, an apron and rather worn-looking lisle stockings of the kind old ladies seem to wear. As she told me moving stories of her past, her vulnerable face would seize up and tears often came to her eyes. She was happy to see me and remembered my family well from the "old, good days." She described to me one of her earliest recollections of those "bad times." She had had a lifelong friendship with a Jewish woman, who, upon her marriage, moved to a nearby town. Frau von

91

Himmel, on a trip to that town to buy some household articles, decided to visit her friend and spend the remainder of the afternoon with her before catching the evening train back to Sonderburg. It was a bright sunny afternoon in late fall of 1933 when she arrived at the door unannounced, as was her custom; her friend opened the door, looked at her in horror, placed her hands on her shoulders and said, "For God's sake, Frieda, leave, don't come in, we are already being watched." They stood at the door, tears came to both their eyes, and Frau Himmel slowly walked away. She said in recounting the incident, "I was stunned, I didn't think there could be anything wrong in visiting an old friend." She cried all the way home. Later she heard that her friend had emigrated to America, and there was never an opportunity to even say good-bye. They never saw each other again.

I met Frau Stefan on the street while walking with another old lady, and, upon being introduced, she immediately recalled that she had gone to school with my younger aunt. As we walked up to the top of the hill where her very comfortable-looking house was situated, she told me that she and her family had recovered after the war and life was fairly happy for her now. Then she reverted to the past, saying that even though she was only ten years old in 1935, she had memories of those times. She recalled how she had always been very friendly with a Jewish butcher and his wife, who were childless. She describes herself as having been virtually adopted by Herr and Frau Meyer and often after school would drop by the shop and receive some sweets. By that year, although the shop was still open, she and other non-Jews could no longer enter it for purchases or visits. One day, early in 1935, she passed the closed window of the shop and saw the butcher standing in front of it looking out onto the street. When he saw her, tears came to his eyes: "Ah, Dutsche [a nickname], you can't come in here again." She went on home wondering all the while why his window was closed and why he had said she couldn't come in. Frau Stefan questioned her mother, who told her, "I don't know why. Herr Meyer is Jewish and we are not supposed to visit Jews anymore. I don't know why, that is what they have told us."

Late in 1934 Frau Karr, thinking that she needed a new dress, walked into Mandel's notions store, where she and her mother had always purchased their dress fabrics. Frau Mandel was a friend of hers and always advised her on the right kind of fabric to buy, the special colors that suited her, and even the style that was most becoming to her. Frau Karr knew that she was not supposed to make purchases in Jewish stores, but she felt she needed the special help that Frau Mandel had always given her. Upon entering the store, she said to Frau Mandel, who was surprised to see her, "I don't care what they say, I need a new dress." Frau Mandel pushed her out of the store saying, "Please, stay out of here, it will do none of us any good." Frau Karr traveled to a nearby town to a department store, where she bought her fabric, wondering why she had to go forty kilometers to buy in a strange store, where her needs were not known by the sales staff. Describing the incident, she recalled that she wondered "what we are all coming to when we can't buy in a store we've patronized all our lives."

For many of the average citizens of Sonderburg, who were accustomed to the many interactions they had with the Jews in their community, Nazi proscriptions against social intercourse with Jews came as a surprise. Some tried to continue their relationships, at least until 1935, despite the prohibitions. For some it was perhaps simply habit, a series of traditions which they found hard to break. Many of the women, in particular, could not understand the reasons for the restrictions against the Jews. "They were part of us, they had always lived here; we grew up together"; how could these traditions be broken overnight because the regime decided they should be broken? It was an incomprehensible situation, and "what had they ever done to us?" was an often repeated refrain. Surprise, incredulity, and disgust were the reactions of Germans, who even then were not happy with the new regime. A few, as in the examples quoted above, tried to maintain some level of interaction with Jews, but as prohibitions increased, particularly with the closing of most Jewish retail shops by 1935, visits to Jews or trading in their shops stopped. There were some exceptions: Herr Tiller and others were still employed in Kahn's department store until late in 1935, and the hundreds of Gentile employees of the Miller factory were in touch with their Jewish bosses until the end of 1938. Interestingly enough, many of the Jews, through fear, rapidly complied with the rules and were the ones to discourage contact with Gentiles. Friendships between women, especially neighbors, were particularly affected and in the course of time disintegrated completely.

Minna had four very close school friends. The five girls were in the same class for years and all were friendly together, forming a sort of social clique. Three of the girls' parents worked for the government, one for the electricity board, one in a legal department and one in the post office. All three had to join the Nazi party early on, and, of necessity, their friendship with Minna ended. She described how one of the girls, Marie, broke up their relationship in 1933:

> She came to me to say good-bye, but how she did it! I was still at work in the Kahn's department store [where she worked until 1935, when it closed], and she sent someone in to tell me to come out, she wanted to talk to me. And she was standing there at one window and I was standing at the other one and she said, "Minna, I'm very, very sorry, I can't talk to you anymore, you are still my friend, but I will lose my livelihood. Just think that I'm a stranger when you see me on the streets because there are so many people around who would see us and I would lose my job." Her mother was a widow by then and needed her support. So it was, one after the other. They had nothing against me as such but they were afraid the SS would come and do something to them, that they kept still and didn't say anything.

In Minna's story, one girlfriend remained in touch because her parents owned a cafe, and, as independent shopkeepers, were not required to join the party. Christina was the only one who retained some contact with her because she was not afraid and because no one in her family had to be a Nazi. This same Christina and her brother later owned a bakery and supplied the remaining Jewish families with bread and rolls, which Christina would deliver secretly to their homes at night.

Jessie described one of her former schoolteachers with whom she was still friendly, although she had graduated from the school years earlier. When Jessie was leaving Sonderburg, "Mrs. Mueller heard I was leaving; the day I left, she was in the Market Place and she called me and said, 'Jessie, they can put me in jail now but I say good-bye to you. I don't care. I'm glad you are leaving and take your family with you because it's no good being here anymore.' In the middle of the Market Place, she said this, she didn't care but if everybody had been like that, those hundred [confirmed Nazis in Sonderburg] would have gone under."

Not only friendships between women were terminated. This is how Joshua Abraham, now in his seventies and living in Manhattan, describes his active social life before the Nazis. We were sitting in his large living room, drinking German cognac while he nostalgically recalled the fun he used to have in the earlier days:

> We all used to play cards together twice a week. I was the only Jew in the circle. The rest were all merchants, one was a stout grocery store owner who was friendly to everybody, another was

a tailor who had one of the best establishments in the town, and we even played with Dansk, who then owned a shoe store [he became the leading Nazi in the town from 1933 until the end of the war]. The game we played was skat and we met in the tavern, drank beer and played for hours. As soon as the Nazis came to power, I was no longer told when they were playing cards. Everything stopped. I would see them on the street and we pretended we didn't see each other. Not one of them spoke to me.

From some of these incidents it would appear that women stopped their relationships with more grace and probably more expressed sorrow, for their partings were far more emotional. Men like Joshua Abraham and his friends, then in their twenties, simply pretended that they no longer knew each other.

John Miller, a tall, well-proportioned man now in his sixties but looking years younger, spoke movingly of what it was like growing up in Sonderburg. His voice was low and he spoke hesitantly, as if these reminiscences were still painful. He noted that he had always played with Gentile children since there were very few Jewish children of his age and grade level. He was in a social clique that also included the friends of his older sister. The group would always play in John Miller's garden, which was very spacious. He and Bertrand were especially friendly:

We were almost inseparable, I would go to his house, he would come to mine and we would do homework together. We did everything together—we were fifteen at the time. One time, in April 1933, I said, "Come on [he had some trouble with school work], let's do it together," and, right in front of my house, he said, "No, I can't anymore, it is forbidden by the Hitler Youth." That hit me very hard and I went to my room and cried for about two days. The next day I went to school, nobody knew about it but I guess my parents recognized the problem although I kept it to myself. At that time I couldn't understand it and I never talked to this boy again, although I stayed at that school for another few months. I saw him again after the war, I recognized him and I suppose he recognized me, but we just acted as if we did not know one another at all.

These instances of broken friendships illustrate how insistent were the regulations prohibiting social intercourse with Jews. For people who had close ties with Jews, particularly school friendships, such prohibitions were difficult to comprehend for both groups, but, of course, they were more severe on the Jews, who felt themselves increasingly isolated. Among schoolchildren, the need to belong to the Hitler Youth meant that many activities formerly shared with Jewish friends were now maintained among Gentiles only. One particularly chilling case involves a Jewish family whose young son had always played with Gentile friends. As they joined the Hitler youth and proudly wore its uniform, the young son cried and asked his mother why he too could not wear such a uniform. His mother felt so sorry for his isolation that she purchased a Hitler Youth uniform and sent him out on the street to play in it and join his friends.

John Miller's story of broken friendship is a particularly good example of isolation. He found his isolation so difficult to bear that he asked his wealthy parents to send him to school abroad. At sixteen, he entered a boarding school in Switzerland but he returned occasionally to Sonderburg for holidays before finally emigrating to the United States in 1936. He movingly describes how on the day of his leaving the Sonderburg school, despite the growing anti-Semitism and social isolation from his former friends, they and some teachers gave him a farewell party:

> Before I left, it was funny, the whole thing was peculiar; nothing was logical, the anti-Semitism, nothing made sense to me. When I said, "I'm going away to school," this was already in the middle of the German school year, they said, "O.K., we will give you a party, a going-away party." And there were all those Gentile boys and girls in the class and we went to a tavern where they illegally served drinks to teen-agers [in a run-down section of the town] and we went and had a few beers. I and the boy I had been friendly with tried to get friendly again but it never worked, it was over. It was a funny feeling but still it happened—it was the beer party for the kid who goes away because he was so isolated.

The growing social and economic isolation of Jews in Sonderburg polarized the German community.[1] Some Gentiles immediately obeyed the edicts and stopped any form of contact even with the Jews whom they knew well. A few, like one of Minna's friends, maintained a degree of friendship, but many simply stopped recognizing Jews when they passed by their homes or saw them on the street. The pretence of nonrecognition, with face down or heads suddenly turning in another direction, was a commonplace experience. Joshua Abraham describes how he behaved when he saw a card-playing friend of his on the street. He quickly crossed over to avoid a direct confrontation, and, he recalls, "We were suddenly nothing, nobody, we no longer existed." A number of people from the community took an active part in the harassment of Jews; they were primarily party members and those who had joined the SA and the SS.

On the other hand, a considerable number of people did not take kindly to the persecution of their neighbors and tried, even in small ways, to offer acts of kindness and resistance. By 1935 all stores had signs in their windows saying "Jews not wanted here," but in several of these shops Jews could still make purchases at night and in secret. Friends and neighbors could also make purchases for them and it was usually known by all concerned that such purchases were made in behalf of Jewish families. The purchases were almost always groceries, meats, and bread. By this time, Jews were no longer buying anything but the necessities for survival. A customer would simply order a number of items, and it was never specified that the extra was for a Jewish family. There appeared to be an unspoken communication between customer and shopkeeper, and extra purchases were never questioned. Otto, a man in his eighties, is today still serving in the family grocery store located on the main street of the town. He had always had a large number of Jewish customers, and, in fact, one Jewish family lived next to his shop. Since the houses were all attached and each looked out into the neighbor's back yard, Frau Loeb would often call from her kitchen window to Otto or his wife and ask for a pound of butter or some milk. He would then bring it up to her or send one of his young boys with it. Otto, along with the other merchants, had the "No Jews wanted here" sign in his window but he always sold goods to his immediate neighbors and others who came by at night. He also knew when a Gentile customer bought extra goods, but no words were ever exchanged. "I sold them as much as I could, more I could not do," he told me in a voice quivering with age and emotion.

Frau Schenk, owner of a variety type of shop, said that she would have allowed Jews to purchase in her store at any time though it might have meant the loss of her other customers. None apparently did so. Photographs were routinely taken of Germans who were buying in Jewish stores as long as they were still legally open—that is, until 1935. Occasionally, the town paper would print pictures of individuals with the caption "This German citizen was seen entering [such and such a] store." One infamous incident involved an old woman who had worked as a cleaner in the Jewish department store for many years. One evening in 1935 she was leaving the store with Herr Kahn, her Jewish employer, and a local SS man stationed across the street snapped their picture in order to incriminate the old woman. When Herr Kahn saw the SS man, he put his arm around the old woman's shoulder and said, "Smile, Frau Schmidt, we are having our picture taken." When the steps of the same store were smeared with excrement night after night, Herr Tiller and a few other employees would arrive early the next morning and clean it off. "Schweine [pigs]," growls Herr Tiller today as he recounts the story. At least until 1935, there was a considerable amount of defiance of regulations among those people who had always had friendly associations with Jews.

Since relations between Jews and Gentiles had been relatively close, the two groups having grown up together and lived in relative harmony, how did these relationships change as Nazism increased its violence against the Jews? The end of many of these relationships has already been described. Certainly, the public aspects of friendships and other ties ceased almost completely. But what happened in private and at night?

In Sonderburg as elsewhere there were Germans who aided Jews, often at great risk to themselves. On the other hand, the vast majority of the population closed its eyes and doors to all things Jewish. Despite these larger numbers who did nothing, a significant minority, perhaps as many as one hundred or more people, did offer aid. Sometimes this amounted to nothing more than, as H.D. Leuner notes, "Good neighbours showing kindness often without committing themselves to any action which could have landed them in trouble."[2]

Acts of Kindness

During the early 1930s, kindness and compassion continued to be shown, and only in dramatic cases were such "offenders" punished. As already noted, Germans were photographed with Jews; furthermore, a blackboard listing those who helped Jews was set up in the central marketplace. More important, however, was the fact that jobs and promotions were almost impossible to attain for those who still had contact with Jews. Thus, even in this early period, subtle means were instituted to humiliate those Germans who kept up a connection with Jews. Later, of course, punishments were more severe, and any help was deemed as traitorous aiding and abetting of Jews, and was cause for arrest of both the helpers and their families—transfers to political concentration camps such as Dachau were commonplace in Germany. Despite these punishments, there were still a few people who helped Jews even after 1939. This was certainly true in Sonderburg since twelve old Jews were kept alive for three years by their German Gentile neighbors and friends. During the earlier period, the most common form of help was the purchase of extra amounts of food, since Jews were no longer allowed to shop. As already noted, these extra amounts of butter, eggs, vegetables, and other supplies were overlooked by shopkeepers, and there was a tacit understanding between shopkeeper and customer that the extra was for Jews. Herr Otto, still a grocer today, described how Frau Schmidt, who had shopped in his store for years, always buying the same items in the same amounts for her family, "suddenly one day asked for two pounds of butter instead of her usual one. I knew of course that the extra pound was for the Mandels, who lived upstairs." Otto himself would bring a supply of groceries from his store to the family Loeb who lived next door to him. The Jewish families, digging into their savings, paid for the purchased goods themselves. Later some of them began bartering household items and sold off their possessions as the financial need arose. Throughout the thirties, Christina and her brother Robert, owners of the bakery, continued baking challah on Friday, which she secretly delivered to Jewish customers late at night. She continued this practice until 1941, not on a weekly basis but whenever she could, so that "they could still celebrate the Friday night meal."

Frau Kramer described how her mother would buy extra rolls and when she walked by the homes of certain Jews, she would throw them through a window left open for just that purpose. The physical and spatial arrangements of this small town abetted such transactions. The ground floor was often on an exact street level so that passersby were level with the window. Many houses in the old sections of the town were terraced and their back gardens joined, separated only by a fence, so that packages were easily tossed over the fence. One person described how her garden and that of her neighbor were joined; the neighbor owned a bakery and she had the "No Jews allowed here" sign prominently displayed in her window, but she would come through the garden gate and call, "Do you need bread? I'll bring it around the back." Frau Bilke, on the other hand, would lead her blind mother across the street every evening so that her mother could visit and bring food to the family across the street.

Frau Kramer's husband encountered the sisters of the Miller family, about to emigrate, while walking down the street one morning. They were struggling to bind a large trunk together and he courteously stopped to help them. This action was seen by Arthur Dansk, a leading Nazi, and reported to the authorities. Three days later Herr Kramer was inducted into the army, even though he was some years older than the average conscript. Herr Tiller was arrested and held in detention for three days because he was overhead making some derogatory comments about the regime. Although many persons said that they feared for their lives, these were the only two acts of retribution that I uncovered in this community. Of course, the news about both of these minor events made the rounds quickly in this small town.

Although Jews were still allowed in the streets and on the public transportation system, Martha described how her friend Lotte insisted on driving her to Frankfurt when she emigrated. They left late at night; Lotte did not dare drive to Martha's house so they met on a small, dead-end street. Martha quickly loaded her goods into the car, and, under cover of darkness, she was driven to the railway station in Frankfurt some two and a half hours away. Lotte felt that this was the least she could do for her friend.

In 1963 my youngest aunt returned to Sonderburg while accompanying her husband on a business trip. Although she did not want to visit Sonderburg, she decided to have at least one look at the home and the town in which she grew up. She found the house still rented to the very tenants who had moved into it in 1936, when Jewish homes were rented to non-Jews while the Jewish owners were forced to live in only one or two rooms. One of the tenants, by then an old woman, greeted my aunt warmly, and showed her inside, saying, "Watch those two little steps there." "I remember them, I grew up here, you know," my aunt replied. The old woman then brought out an old box filled with Hebrew books, which my grandfather had left in her care. He told her on the morning of his deportation to keep the books safe because one day one of his children might return to Sonderburg. My aunt was moved to see that they were all prayer books that had been in the family for many generations. The tenant had kept them secretly during all those years, when even the presence of Hebrew books in her home would have been an indictment against her. A small act, perhaps, but one that led to the recovery of books having great sentimental value to the family.

Another act of kindness also involved religious books. During the Kristallnacht pogrom, the synagogue in Sonderburg was burned. An unidentified Gentile man who worked for the town was able to rescue seven Torahs from the building either before it was actually burned or shortly thereafter. He apparently kept them in his possession until 1945, when Sonderburg was occupied by the French army and he turned them over to the French military. One was kept for use by a Jewish rabbi in the French army and the remainder were sent to the United States. In the United States, two of them came into the possession of Mr. Miller, who eventually donated them to a synagogue in New York. The man who kept them hidden may well have been a supporter of Jews or perhaps he was angered by acts of desecration against religious articles. Although that synagogue is now a warehouse, at least its most precious possessions were saved through the generous act of one individual.

The most dramatic example of aid was that given to the twelve Jews who remained in Sonderburg until they were deported to Theresianstadt in July 1942. Old Mr. Miller lived fairly well, for his Gentile housekeeper remained with him until the very end. Eleven others living in straitened circumstances fared less well. Most could occupy only one or two rooms in their homes and their entire food supply came from friends and neighbors. Secret parcels of food were left at their doorsteps, or thrown through windows or across fences; in this way they were able to survive for three years. (It is worth noting here that when I spoke to surviving relatives of these Jews and asked how their parents kept alive, they would say "Well, of course, people would bring them food, they had good friends who looked after them," even though only minutes later or earlier these same individuals condemned all Germans, often with the phrase "They were all Nazis, every single one of them!") Although Frau Bilke's mother still paid visits, she was apparently one of the few to do so. The other Jews rarely had German visitors, and they did not visit each other often. Word-of-mouth information passed through the small group, but they rarely ventured out. Nevertheless, they were kept alive in the community, only to lose their lives in concentration camps some years later.

One might have expected the churches to pay some heed to the sufferings of Jews. This was not the case. The only aid given was on an individual rather than institutional basis. Institutionally, both the Catholic and Protestant churches failed the Jews in their hour of direst need. They failed to protest publicly against the persecution and mass murder until it was too late; they even helped the state by providing extracts from their baptismal records to prove German or Jewish descent.[3] In Sonderburg, I could find no evidence that either the Protestant churches, of which there were several, or the single Roman Catholic church ever did anything publicly to help Jews. (The single exception to this was the incident noted earlier, where the minister admonished the Nazi informer there to spy on his sermon). Two ministers with whom I spoke had been installed there only recently and knew nothing of the earlier period. None of my informants could recall anything about the role of the churches, except one old lady, who said, "You had to be careful even in church."

Why did these few people perform acts of kindness while others did not? This question is difficult to answer because on the surface nothing distinguished Christina, her brother, or Frau Bilke's mother from anyone else in the town. They were all lower-middle class or upper-working class people; their homes, jobs, and incomes in no way differed from those of their neighbors. Nor were they any more or any less religious than others. Christina and Minna were very close friends but Christina's brother was not especially friendly with any Jews. When I first met him in the hotel dining room, he was in no way different from any of the men around the table. He looked like them, older, graying, slightly stooped. He spoke like them and drank as heartily as they did. It was when he described to me how he or his sister would drop off the bakery goods at Jewish homes that his voice quavered. When I asked why he had done that, he remained silent for a moment and finally responded in almost a plaintive voice, "But we always made challah for the Jews, even in my parents' time. They needed it for their Sabbath."

Frau Bilke's mother was a close friend of the Jewish family that lived across the street, but most of the people who delivered the food packages were neighbors not especially friendly with the Jews. It was the inhumanity directed against the Jews that stirred their compassion. For some perhaps, as for Robert the baker, the forces of tradition ("we always did it so") were sufficient to make them act as charitable Christians toward their Jewish neighbors. Most of the people who aided Jews had worked for Jews or had long neighborhood ties with them. They had lived in close proximity to Jewish families. The former employees of Jews felt that they had always been treated well by their employers. They were mainly lower-middle- to middle-class people, close in class level to the majority of the Jewish families so that relationships were cemented by common ties of social class as well as neighborhood proximity. These people did not like the regime and were against its maltreatment of the Jews. Accordingly, they tried in small ways to give as much aid as possible.

A number of sources indicate that there was considerable resistance to Nazism in general and to the anti-Semitic measures in particular. R. Birley notes, for example that, despite the fact that no organized resistance movement was possible in a totalitarian state, there were many pockets of opposition in the factories and among trade unionists.[4] Some writers and journalists, such as Rudolf Pechel, who survived imprisonment, also offered resistance. A secret society of students at the University of Munich, known as the White Rose, distributed anti-Nazi pamphlets, but their leaders were executed in 1943. Small student movements existed in other universities as well. Individual members of the Protestant and Catholic churches took heroic stands against Nazism. Examples include the famous bishop of Münster, von Galen; and the two Protestant pastors, Martin Niemöller and Dietrich Bonhoeffer. Politicians, intellectuals and members of the clergy composed the Kreisau Circle— a group of dissidents who often met in Kreisau, Silesia. T. Prittie also notes that there was not much in the way of formal, organized resistance but that the "Germans who opposed Hitler had, very often, little hope of earthly profit or recognition. What they did was done at the dictates of their conscience."[5] Specific resistance to anti-Semitism occurred primarily in the larger cities, where members of the Jewish communities were hidden by Gentile neighbors. In Berlin about 50,000 Jews were hidden during the war, and many acts of kindness occurred there, including the famous "Uncle Emil" network of underground helpers.[6] Some Germans have been honored in Israel by the awarding of the Yad Vashem medal. (Yad Vashem is a memorial to the dead of the Holocaust. Included in its grounds is the Avenue of the Righteous of Nations, composed of rows of trees, each one honoring a Christian who aided a Jew. Many Germans are included in the avenue.) Sarah A. Gordon notes that both anti-Semitism and the resistance to it changed with the times. Early in the 1930s attitudes toward Jews were more favorable, but in the mid-decade a minority of the population, mostly party members, applauded racial persecution while another minority opposed it. "These two minorities were probably polarized around an acquiescent majority."[7] By 1938, anti-Semitism was again stronger but was somewhat dispelled by the violence and destruction of Kristallnacht which even the majority opposed.

Dramatic acts such as hiding Jews did not occur in Sonderburg, but, as was shown earlier in this chapter, a minority of its population did aid Jews in small ways. People who helped Jews were classified by the regime as *Judenfreunde* (friends of Jews). What accounts of the *Judenfreunde* often lack is an explanation of what motivated them to help. There is at least one source that describes the socio-economic characteristics of those who aided Jews, but it too cannot explain the problem of motivation.

Gordon analyzed Gestapo files from the district of Dusseldorf, which included 452 cases of individual opposition to racial persecution. Of these 203 individuals who aided Jews, 24 were critics of racial persecution and 30 were only suspected of aiding Jews. The remainder had or were alleged to have had sexual contacts with Jews. These *Rassenschänder*, or those who had sex with Jews in contravention of the Nuremberg racial laws, were primarily middle-class younger men. Most contacts between Jews and non-Jews occurred between 1935 and 1937. Jews gained the strongest support in 1938–39 and during the actual war years. The majority of those who supported Jews were men, but in later years women were also included in this category. Gordon's analysis reveals that men who were residents of large cities and either independent businessmen or white-collar workers supported Jews or had sexual contacts with them out of proportion to their actual numbers in the population. Conversely, women, blue-collar workers, and farmers were underrepresented among those who helped Jews.[8] Gordon's findings are consistent with those of others, who note that more men than women tended to aid Jews.

Although the present sample is very small, my impression is that in Sonderburg more women than men helped Jews. This is probably due to the fact that most of the aid given involved the provision of food—women's work, as opposed to administrative help with papers, passports and the like, which is associated with men. Given the size of the community and the face-to-face relations that most people engaged in before Hitler's rise to power, hiding Jews or even helping them to escape would have been impossible. The fact that the statistical analysis of a larger sample elsewhere in Germany indicates a predominance of men suggests to Gordon that women were also likely to be more anti-Semitic. My hypothesis, however, is that in small communities women's help was more important for survival. In larger urban areas, perhaps the administrative type of help that men could supply might have been more crucial. But the data from Sonderburg on age are consistent with Gordon's study. In general, non-Jews over the age of forty were the Jews' main helpers. Frau Bilke, Kramer, and others discussed the help their mothers—then women in their early forties—gave to the Jews in Sonderburg.

My findings also concur with Gordon's in that almost all supporters of Jews in Sonderburg were middle class. As suggested earlier, the fact that most of the Jews were middle class meant that their strongest associations were with similarly placed middle-class Gentiles. (Gordon suggests that the working class was underrepresented amongst *Judenfreunde* because it simply did not have the means or the money to help the Jews. My present sample is too small for me to comment on this hypothesis.)

In the Dusseldorf files analyzed by Gordon, actual prison and concentration camp internment was the fate of those found guilty of being *Judenfreunde* or *Rassenschänder*. These extreme measures were not taken in Sonderburg, although there were the two cases of punishment mentioned earlier. It is also highly probable that there were sexual contacts between Jews and Gentiles as late as 1938 or 1939 since there were at least two Sonderburg women who were involved with non-Jews, but the incidents did not result in imprisonment for the men.

While the socioeconomic characteristics of Jewish supporters are worthy of study, these analyses tell us little about the individual motivations. Why did one person help Jews while his or her immediate neighbor of the same class standing did not? My explanation for Sonderburg, as noted above, is that work ties and neighborhood contacts were the predisposing factors that led some people to help Jews. That this is not a total explanation is obvious when one recalls that some immediate neighbors were, in fact, committed members of the Nazi party. For example, if we examine closely just one segment of a neighborhood in Sonderburg, the results indicate that some helped and others did not. On lower Grossestrasse, Otto's grocery and residence was directly next to the fabric store of the Mandels, whose residence was behind their shop. A few houses from the grocery, lived the von Himmel family, and, immediately next to it, the Pilkens. Next to them were the Muellers. Directly across the street lived the Bilkes and the Kurts, who owned a variety shop, and immediately opposite to them were my grandparents.

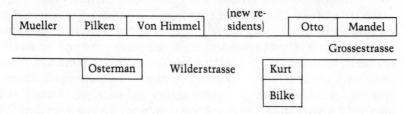

Mueller	Pilken	Von Himmel	(new residents)	Otto	Mandel

Grossestrasse

	Osterman	Wilderstrasse	Kurt
			Bilke

Otto sold groceries to the Jews and those who bought for them and secretly sent supplies next door to the Mandels. The Bilkes

regularly brought food parcels to my grandparents. The von Him-
mels, while not giving aid, were always sympathetic and ready to
greet their neighbors, but both the Pilkens and the Muellers were
early and rabid Nazi supporters. In the Pilken household, Herr
Pilken was one of the earliest joiners, but Frau Pilken never joined
the party. Even amongst the Bilkes, the youngest son became an SS
officer while his mother and sister gave food parcels to the Jews—
food that Herr Bilke would obtain from his farmer relatives. Thus
even neighborhood contacts are an insufficient explanation in dis-
tinguishing Nazis from *Judenfreunde*. In the final analysis, it may
well be that some persons were simply more humane than others.

In general terms, the population of Sonderburg can be divided
into three groups. There were approximately several hundred persons of the kind we have been describing as sympathetic to the Jews;
these were counterbalanced by about one hundred firm and committed Nazis (see Chapter 1); between these two extremes was the
remainder of the population, which was by and large apathetic toward the Jewish issue and which obeyed the regulations and edicts
of the Nazi regime. These people kept their mouths shut and their
thoughts to themselves, and they did nothing to disturb the status
quo.

Legal and Social Prohibitions Against Jews

The exclusion of the Jews from the mainstream of German
society began early in 1933.[9] The first series of laws excluded them
from the civil service and the legal profession. This was quickly
followed by laws excluding Jews from the medical and dental profession and the cultural fields of art, music, literature, and later journalism. By the end of April, a special law supposedly designed to
alleviate the overcrowding in German schools reduced the number
of Jewish students to a minimum. By the end of 1933, "public life
had virtually been cleared of Jews and other non-Aryans."[10] The
majority of Jews in commerce and trade continued to make their
livelihood in these areas, which were as yet unregulated. The early
laws had little effect in Sonderburg since there were no Jewish civil
servants, professionals, or artists. Insofar as my respondents recall,
there was never a Jewish journalist either. One noteworthy exception, however, was the synagogue leader and religious teacher, who
also held a post in the public school system. Joshua Abraham had
been hired by the synagogue community in 1928, and he and his

wife took up residence in Sonderburg. Soon after, he was hired as a public school teacher—a position he held until 1933. He describes his work and social condition during this period as being agreeable. He found the officials extremely helpful and cooperative: "They helped me in every way when I got there. They introduced me to the Catholic priest and the Protestant minister and to all the other teachers. I was welcomed into the group. I went to the teachers' association which got together every month. The director of my school was very nice. I was trying to do an additional exam and he helped me in every way to further myself and my education." Although Abraham was aware of some anti-Semitism in the teachers' association, he says that it did not endanger him at first:

> Already in the 20s there were a few members who started to talk against the Jews, but my other colleagues always defended me. At a large open meeting of teachers for the whole area, hundreds of teachers were there, a couple got up and started talking against the Jews, or against me because I was the only Jewish chap in that association. Then the director got up and defended me and said, "I know Mr. Abraham, and I won't allow any discrimination against him." That was in 1932. A little later, the following year, the same director called me into his office and said, "Abraham, I have to let you go because that is my official order."

Mr. Abraham also had had friendly social ties in the town and he claims that as a religious leader he was treated with particular cordiality and respect. At the various shops, notably in the cigar store, where he was a regular customer, he was always courteously hailed as "teacher Abraham." All of this changed very rapidly. "Before I met people on the street, they talked to me, they greeted me, wished me well. Afterward nobody knew me." He recalls that early in 1933 he witnessed the first SS parade in Sonderburg.

> They marched by and I, by accident, stood by the window and they must have seen me and they sent up a young SS man. The man was young, about 18 or 19, from the tailor shop where I had my suits made. I knew him and his father, the tailor, very well. And he knew me and said to me, "Mr. Abraham, I was sent up by my leader, you have to get away from the window or they will arrest you. I personally have to excuse myself, but I have to follow orders." I said, "Don't excuse yourself, I understand your position."

After his dismissal from his teaching position, he resigned from the synagogue and left Sonderburg to join his wife's family in her home town, about thirty miles away, in order to await their emigration papers. He explains his move saying that he felt more secure in his wife's town and no longer trusted the situation in Sonderburg, where he felt "they were after me." Mr. Abraham decided to emigrate immediately—it was the abruptness of his job dismissal that led to his decision to leave the country as soon as his papers were in order. Mr. Abraham was one of the first in this community to fully understand the precarious nature of Jewish existence in Germany. Perhaps he grasped the situation more quickly because he was a public school teacher and the only Jewish civil servant, and as such was fired very soon after the regime came to power. Most other Jews, who were self-employed, never experienced the trauma of being fired for no other reason than that of being Jewish. He was also quick to understand the necessity of following orders and felt no personal animosity toward either the tailor's son or his own director who fired him, since he knew that they were simply following orders and had lost their personal freedom to act with decency.

While most of the Jews in Sonderburg were self-employed, there were also some, mostly in their late teens and early twenties, who were employed by others. Three of them were working in Kahn's department store but lost their jobs when that store was forced to close in 1935. A few worked in Miller's factory, and another four or five people worked outside of Sonderburg since the employment possibilities there, particularly at the onset of the depression, were fairly limited. Alice worked as a hairdresser in Frankfurt but lost her job in 1934, when the owner of the shop regretfully told her that he could no longer keep her on since "it might get me in trouble." She was able to emigrate to the United States one year later. Another young woman went to Munich, where she was employed as a sales clerk until 1934. Mr. Albert moved to a town in the Ruhr Valley in 1930 and there worked as a sales clerk in a furniture store. His employers held him in high regard and he was given a raise in salary one year later. On April 21, 1933, a few months after Hitler was proclaimed chancellor, Mr. Albert received the following letter from the owner of the business:

April 21, 1933

Mr. A. Albert
Pfefferackerstr, 40
Buer.

Until today we have been trying to keep you in our employ by merely putting you into temporary retirement, i.e., we gave you a leave of absence, even though it has caused us immense problems because of your Jewish extraction. Unfortunately, the present state of affairs can no longer be sustained and the development of things forces us today to take grave measures.

Under the prevailing circumstances, it will be impossible that you continue to perform your present duties with us in the future. It would otherwise be most detrimental to our company.

These reasons force us to take the sad measures herewith to revoke, without notice, our contractual relationship. We understand the extraordinary severity this must imply for you. However, under the given circumstances, we have no other choice and you will surely appreciate our precautions, if you put yourself in our situation.

In order to facilitate your position, we are prepared to give you your present salary, as agreed to in our contract, for this month and the month of May, at the end of each month respectively.

Yours truly,

THEODOR BEHR

What is particularly interesting about this letter is that it expressed considerable regret at the need to terminate Mr. Albert's employment, recognizing the "severity this must imply" for him and offering another month's severance pay. Up to this point, he had already been in his position of "temporary retirement" for one month. The letter is also fairly detailed and lengthy, perhaps indicating the discomfort the writer felt in pursuing this action. In theory, at least, a revocation of an employment contract could have been stated in two sentences. The writer's unease is also suggested by the frequent use of euphemisms such as "the development of things" and "under the prevailing circumstances." Jewish extraction could safely be mentioned, but in writing, the sociopolitical environment created by Nazism could only be alluded to. There is also an ironic twist to the suggestion that "you will surely appreciate our precautions, if you put yourself in our situation." As if there existed even the remotest possibility that such a reversal could take place!

Other early anti-Semitic laws included the Enabling Act of March 1933, which established the first concentration camps, including the notorious Dachau near Munich, which was used to detain dissenters of all kinds, as well as Jews. Acts of violence against

Jews were initiated early in 1933. In Sonderburg, few incidents of actual violence occurred, but, again, there was one major exception. One Jew was arrested and sent to a concentration camp as early as 1933, and although no official reasons were given for his arrest, it was widely suspected that besides being Jewish, he was also a member of the Communist party. He never returned, but the Nazis kindly sent back his ashes.

The first official boycott of Jewish shops took place on April 1, 1933. This boycott was not especially successful in all of Germany nor in the small towns. In Sonderburg, many people were not even aware of the boycott and shopped as usual. By and large, the first official legislation against Jews had little effect in the small community of Sonderburg, since almost no one was directly affected by it.

Unofficially, of course, anti-Semitic behavior started to occur as early as 1933, although, as noted in Chapter 3, there had been anti-Semitic actions in this town much earlier. The most obvious example, described earlier, was the way in which people who had been friendly severed all connections with each other. They would pass each other by on streets without even making eye contact. From 1933 onward, incidents of harassment began occurring with some regularity, and were committed by those who were already Nazis. For example, Albert, a man now in his late seventies, recalled vehemently how his friendship with Rudy ended: "We grew up together, he lived around the corner from me. I was at his house, he was at mine. We went through the whole *Realschule* [high school] together and when I came back to Sonderburg in 1934, he passed me on the street, stopped, spat in my face and called me *dreckiger Jud* [dirty Jew]."

My mother related an experience that took place in 1933. She was walking down a street in Sonderburg, wheeling me, then a very small child, in a baby carriage. On turning a corner, she was accosted by a group of youths who shouted at her, "Here comes the dirty whore who goes to bed with a Jew and has the nerve to wheel around her bastard." This comment referred to the fact that my mother, born and raised Protestant, converted to Judaism upon marrying my father. Another example also involved my own family. My father returned to Sonderburg in 1933 for a period of time before opening a medical practice in the nearby town of Kreuzen. In Sonderburg, he treated mainly Jewish patients but also a number of Gentiles. The Gentile patients were mainly those who lived close to the family home, had always known "young Willem," and were pleased that he had gone away to study medicine. (Frau Bilke told me that she and her parents were still being treated by my father as late as 1934–35. She laughed as she recalled her particular childhood ailments that he treated; the treatments included some form of physiotherapy for her bowed legs!) One night, well past midnight, the doorbell to the family home rang. Thinking it might be a patient in distress, my uncle opened the door to find Herr Dansk, the *Ortsgruppenleiter*, in full Nazi SS regalia. Dansk told him to give a message to his brother: "Tell the so-called Herr Doktor that he is not fit to heal pigs!" Having delivered his message, he turned and walked away.

In another case, Mr. Martin described how he was waiting in line at the town hall in order to fill out some documents. As his turn came to approach the wicket, a man roughly pushed him back, shouting, "Dirty Jew, get to the back of the line." And, in a similar situation, a gang of young Nazis encountering two Jewish men about to enter town hall jumped them and began beating them until both managed to escape, but with severe head wounds. Several other town residents watched this incident but none came to the aid of the outnumbered Jews.

John Miller relates that in the spring of 1934 a group of Jewish boy scouts from Mainz came to his door and asked for accommodation for the night. His father put them up in an empty building, which belonged to the factory. "Shortly, there was a commotion," he recalls "a few people had been mobilized to stone the building where these kids of ten, eleven, and twelve years of age were housed. I went after the police but they were reluctant to come. I remember standing outside the building and the people were stoning and there was the father of my best friend egging them on to throw more stones." Later that year he was standing in front of the gate of his own home when "a big guy, he may have been nineteen or twenty, comes by and says, 'You're a Jew,' and he slapped me left and right in the face and walked off. He was not a local but with somebody who was. My father did complain about that, and some apology came, but what difference would it make from there on."

While the early official pronouncements had little effect in Sonderburg on a day-to-day basis, acts of harassment such as verbal slurs and direct physical attacks on Jews did take place. These acts were, in the main, perpetrated by those who had already become hard-core Nazis. The passive majority did not actually attack Jews but, as noted above, they merely stopped all interaction with Jews.

By 1935 the regime entered a new phase in its oppression of the

Jews by enacting the Nuremberg race laws. This legislation changed the status of Jews from that of citizen to "subject" and, in order to keep German blood pure, prohibited intermarriage and sexual intercourse between Jews and non-Jews. In addition, Jews were defined by reference to the paternal line, that is whether their fathers, grandfathers, etc., were Jews. The category of *Mischling*, or mixed blood, was introduced. Furthermore, non-Jewish domestics under the age of fifty could no longer be employed in Jewish households (this presumably because Jewish males were seducers and given to attacking their domestic servants!).

In a small community such as Sonderburg, these laws were paid little heed since few people were directly affected by them. Again, however, there were some exceptions. As already noted in Chapter 3, despite the national trend toward intermarriage in the larger cities, there were few such cases in Sonderburg. Among the residents, there was one intermarried couple who had been together for many years and were undisturbed by the legislation—in all likelihood because the family was very prominent in the town and belonged to the small upper class. Its economic and social position at the top of the town hierarchy meant that, despite the new laws, both the residents and even the SS turned a blind eye toward it. In another case, a couple who lived just at the outskirts of the town in a nearby village was similarly protected. The wife was one of only three Jews in that village and her husband belonged to a well-known family whose origins went back several centuries. These isolated cases suggest that, in small communities where the number of mixed marriages was very small, the Nuremberg race laws were not taken seriously. However, where a young couple was concerned—young people who were not married but merely going together—the laws did have their desired effect. In one instance, the daughter of a fairly prominent middle-class Jewish family had a Gentile suitor from another town. Both parties and their families agreed that marriage was not possible since it would have contravened the law. The Jewish woman emigrated, but her suitor was unable to leave the country with her, and, in a tragic and ironic twist of fate, was later sent to a concentration camp as an intellectual dissenter. He eventually died there. Another young Jewish woman asked her Gentile boyfriend to emigrate with her—"Come with me, I'm going"—but he too was unable to secure an exist visa, thus ending that relationship. (Gentiles without relatives abroad were also barred from leaving Hitler's Germany). In one other case, a young Jewish woman from a neighboring village who worked and boarded in Sonderburg also had a Gentile boyfriend, but "they wouldn't let us marry." Today she recalls that when she met with one of her former girlfriends during a visit to Germany, she was told that her former suitor had married on the rebound after her emigration but did not find happiness with his wife. When Alice, another young Jewish woman, married a Jew from another community shortly before emigration, she heard that her ex-suitor, while expressing happiness about her leaving, hoped that her new husband would "take care of me properly."

It is perhaps not commonly known that the regime was almost as hard on Germans who wished to emigrate as it was on Jews. While it appears that very few wished to emigrate, nevertheless, the few who would have left to join their Jewish sweethearts were prevented from doing so. The German government at the time probably did not look kindly on those who might wish to leave, particularly men who might be needed in the party and most certainly later in the armed forces.

Thus, there were a few instances in the younger generation where love was found to be politically unacceptable and where relationships were destroyed as a result of the repressive situation. Although only four such incidents came to light in this study, it is worth speculating as to the effect of these broken ties on the lives of the people involved. In the case of Alice, her former suitor married on the rebound and endured a less than satisfactory marriage. Minna remained single until the age of forty-nine, when she entered into a comfortable, companionable marriage. Martha, who had been involved with a Catholic intellectual dissenter, also remained unmarried until her early forties; her former boyfriend died in Dachau. And Minna's parents, belonging to an earlier generation, whose youth predated the Nuremberg race laws, had nevertheless been discouraged from marrying their sweethearts and joined in an unhappy marriage. While it is dangerous to generalize, it would appear that some of these individuals lived unhappily in their subsequent marriages, and several of the women waited for many years before marrying at a much later age than usual. A pattern of disturbed relationships does seem to have occurred for those whose youthful romances were altered by the course of history.

One other example bears mentioning. The old patriarch of the Miller family, the wealthiest Jewish family in the town, had had a Protestant housekeeper in his employ for many years. She remained his housekeeper throughout the thirties although her friends and family urged her to leave, particularly after the enactment of the

Nuremberg laws. She had worked in that family from the time she was a very young girl and indeed was considered part of the family. Since the old man had been a bachelor all of his life, there was some speculation that the relationship was more than one of employer and employee. They were closely attached to each other, as revealed in his letters quoted in Chapter 4. Throughout the thirties, she shopped for food and groceries and, although it was known that she was shopping for a Jew, no one gave her any trouble and she moved freely about the town, often bringing the old man news of latest developments. Her attachment ended only when the old man was deported in 1942. On the day he was taken away, she gave him a postcard addressed to herself with the instructions that as soon as he arrived to where he was being taken he should mail the card so that she would know that he was well and had arrived safely. She apparently did not suspect that he would be taken to a camp and killed there. Like other Germans, she still believed that Jews were being taken to labor camps or to Poland, as though a ninety-four-year-old man would have had any laboring contribution to make. She inherited his home and some money, and is still maintained in an old-age home by the Miller family. She is now in her nineties herself.

The race laws affected not only intermarried Jews but also those who had converted to Christianity. At least two such persons lived in Sonderburg during the 1920s, but they left the town and their fate could not be determined.

With only a few exceptions, then, official acts of legal persecution had little effect on this small community. The business restrictions had a more severe impact. By 1935 only a few shops remained open, and from then until 1938, when the large Jewish firm was closed, Jews were not able to conduct much business except among themselves and with the few Gentile customers who might still make purchases for them in secret. Shop owners sold their premises for very little money and they and others began selling off articles of furniture, jewelry, and other possessions in order to survive. Jewish families forced to sell off their possessions did so in the town whenever possible but more often went to the nearby city of Kreuzen for the purpose. The Kahn department store had employed a number of younger Jews, but the firm was sold and its owners emigrated in 1935. Before then it traded off non-Jewish employees to Gentile business establishments in exchange for Jewish employees. As mentioned earlier, Helen, who had worked for a Gentile firm, was given a job in the Jewish-owned department store in exchange for one of its non-Jewish employees, who took Helen's former job. Several such exchanges took place, especially involving young employees who were awaiting their papers to emigrate. While they waited, some were still able to earn money by being exchanged into the two remaining Jewish-owned firms. The largest firm remained in business until 1938 and the vast majority of its workers were non-Jews. By 1938 official decrees proclaimed that all Jewish firms were to close or be bought out by Germans, often very cheaply. By December 1938 all former Jewish concerns were "aryanized."

The last major form of oppression that assaulted the Jewish population prior to actual deportations occurred on November 9, 1938: the infamous Kristallnacht. Unlike previous measures, it affected the lives of the remaining Jewish residents of Sonderburg in dramatic and, indeed, tragic ways.

On November 7, 1938, a young Jewish student shot and killed an official of the German embassy in Paris. The assassination gave the Nazis an excuse to stage a massive pogrom against the Jews that involved the destruction of Jewish homes, properties, synagogues, and cemeteries. The affair was supposed to be a spontaneous outbreak of the populace against the Jews, but, in fact, it was a carefully stage-managed attack, led and carried out primarily by SA and SS members under orders from the central regime. In Sonderburg as elsewhere, the local SA, with its ranks swollen by those who came from other localities, carried out massive destruction against Jewish property. Herr Otto, today in his eighties, remembers how the troops were marshaled and organized.

> All members of the SS were asked to meet in the square behind the town hall, sympathizers were also called out to the meeting. I was not in the SS but I went to see what was happening. About a hundred men were there. Dansk said that the provocation from the Jews was no longer to be tolerated, we are going to teach them a lesson, tonight we are going to show them who is boss. Then he and his assistants divided the crowd into groups of five, and each group was told to go to a certain number of houses with instructions to destroy everything. Special groups were assigned to the cemetery and the synagogue. I went home right away and a number of other men also sneaked away.

In Sonderburg the synagogue was partially destroyed and burned and its windows smashed. Most of the headstones in the cemetery were broken and toppled over. Although elsewhere in the country, thousands of Jews were rounded up and sent to concentration camps the morning after Kristallnacht and several hundred were killed, there was no loss of life or immediate deportation in Sonderburg. In this small community, these events created confusion and alarm among the very population that was supposed to be carrying out the raids. Eyewitnesses and others could not understand what was taking place and most responded by staying within their homes, doors locked and window shades pulled down. No one interfered with the proceedings, but many people in the secrecy of their homes felt alarm and apprehension, and some event wept to think of what was occurring in Jewish homes.

Irmgard, then seventeen, who lived directly across the street from a Jewish family with whom her parents were friendly, reported that she was awakened by loud noises when suddenly a porcelain pitcher was hurled from the window of the Jewish house through her own and landed on the floor of her bedroom. She and her family got up, put on the lights, and ran downstairs. When they saw a group of SS men destroying the Jewish home, they quickly withdrew and kept very quiet. She went back to sleep but remembers that her parents remained awake for the rest of the night, wondering if such an attack might come to them since they were not party members. The next evening her father, who was a carpenter, went over to the ravaged house and mended broken furniture so that the family could still live in some comfort. Herr Mauer also witnessed Kristallnacht. He remembers walking past a rich Jewish house on his way home that evening. He saw an SS man carrying out a large radio, "the best and most expensive radio in the town," followed by the old man of the family shouting, "I'll give it to you but please don't break it up," as the SS man smashed it to the ground. As Herr Mauer fled home, he had to pass a small alley leading to the outskirts of the city. There he saw about ten or twenty Jews, some holding bandages to bleeding heads, running down the alley trying to flee from the devastation. Again, Herr Mauer did not even try to intervene but locked his doors and windows as soon as he arrived home.

Frau Kramer recalls her mother coming home that evening with tears in her eyes and saying to her father, "They're in Mandels', Loebs' and other houses, throwing everything out the window. The street is full of feathers [from the feather comforters that were ripped open and dumped out the windows]. Why are they doing this? What did they [the Jews] do to us?" Her father made sure that the door was secured.

Another eyewitness remembers seeing Frau Mandel come screaming out of her store, blood dripping down her face as she ran down the street. He notes that "I wanted to go across and help her but what could I do? They would have come after me too." Herr Tiller, one of the kindest people toward Jews in Sonderburg, knew that an old couple fled their home in the early morning of Kristallnacht to take refuge in the nearby village of Stattheim with a sister and her Gentile husband. Tiller saw them again two hours later, after they had been taken from the sister's home and forced to run through the streets of Sonderburg, followed by a gang of SA throwing stones and hurling abuse at them. By then even Tiller was afraid to come to their assistance.

A considerable number of Jews had already left Sonderburg by this time so that there are only a few today who experienced Kristallnacht and are able to describe it. Minna and her parents were still there, and she describes what happened in her home:

> It was around six o'clock in the morning when five young fellows came in. Four whom I didn't know were from Steinhardt and one was from Sonderburg who had worked with me at Kahn's department store for at least ten years. He didn't do anything, he only sent the others in and they destroyed everything in the room. They came to me as I stood there, they told me to go to the window, then they came with an axe but instead of hitting me, they hit the windows. A couple of hours later, the schoolchildren came by and threw stones in. My father had a heart attack in the kitchen so they didn't come in there but the living room was all a mess. My mother ran out into the garden. The man who worked with me said nothing; I looked at him and he looked at me but he lowered his face. Among the four was the veterinarian [an early and well-known Nazi official] and he came to my father's bedroom and said "Mein Herr, following orders from above, we must destroy your house. You and your wife, go out."

Minna believes that the veterinarian said this as an apology since he was her father's superior in World War I and he had known him well through some sporting activities they had in common. She does not know whether he apologized to other families. (In an ironic footnote, this same veterinarian wrote to her father in New York after the war asking for an affidavit to prove that he was not a Nazi. Needless to say, her father did not respond to his request.)

Another woman who experienced the event was at that time only eleven years old, but her memory of Kristallnacht remains "as if it happened yesterday." She recalls hearing loud footsteps on the wooden stairs leading to her house, the wooden doors were hammered open and "men were standing there with axes in their hands, all dressed in black. They ran around axing all our furniture and throwing things out the window. They smashed the closet door and broke all my toys. Afterward, we hid in a closet in a neighbor's apartment."

Hildegard Miller remembers them pounding down the door to her home. Furniture was smashed, the destruction carried out by people she did not know. Later she was told that one of the attackers was a worker in her father's factory. Her mother was alarmed and distraught and ran around trying to calm her children, telling them in her confusion, "Never mind, the insurance will pay for it."

Some noteworthy facts emerged from these accounts. Jewish men obviously attempted to fight back their aggressors, as is evidenced by the number of bleeding heads and bandages eyewitnesses saw. These physical attacks must have occurred when the man of the house tried to bar the Nazis' entry into the house. Frau Mandel was attacked when she attempted to remove a precious article from her store. One man was hit on the head when he tried to close the door on the entering Nazis. There were attempts at resistance on the part of the Jews during Kristallnacht, although it is often alleged that Jews did not fight back.

The German reaction to the pogrom was one of surprise and fear for their own lives and property. People who had had good contacts with Jews were especially upset by the destruction, but they felt powerless to intervene in behalf of their neighbors. They feared retribution against themselves and some were unsure if the pogrom was to be carried out only against Jews. Frau Himmel and others thought that their homes would be attacked too, and she said to her husband, "We are going to be next; maybe we should join the party, too."

In recounting these events, several Germans said that for them the saddest part of Kristallnacht was watching the SS the next morning forcing Jews, some on their hands and knees, to sweep up the broken furniture, feathers, and glass that littered the streets. "I cried when I saw old Mr. Miller, a man of ninety, pushing a broom back and forth in front of his house while a group of young SS stood around and laughed."

For the Jews who had remained in Sonderburg out of choice or necessity, Kristallnacht was the final blow. Those in business who had hesitated about leaving their property and their country made the long-withheld decision immediately. Although several of the younger Millers had already emigrated by then, the senior Millers were still running the factory. After Kristallnacht, although their factory was not touched (specific orders forbade the destruction of this major money-making concern, where hundreds of Gentile people were still employed), the remaining Miller family (with the exception of the patriarch) left as quickly as they could. They sold the factory at well below market prices. While some Jews remained only because they had no emigration papers or no American quota numbers, others remained until 1938 by choice when they had major business interests such as the Millers'. As one man put it, "Even up to then, we didn't believe it could happen. We thought the worst was over. They couldn't kill us, we were Germans after all. But Kristallnacht changed my mind, I left in 1939." In retrospect, such trust in being German seems ludicrous in the face of the continued anti-Semitic barrage issued by the regime, but this view underestimates the commitment and patriotism that Jews even in a small town felt toward their country.

Although earlier legislative assaults against the Jewish community did not have a significant impact on Jews in Sonderburg, large numbers of them emigrated during the mid- and late 1930s. The final assault—but not yet the final solution—was the devastation of Kristallnacht.

As of 1939, only twelve Jews remained in Sonderburg. They included four members of the Hardt family: two older brothers, Milton and George, aged seventy-six and seventy-four; Milton's wife Barbara, aged sixty-six; and their seventy-three-year-old sister-in-law. All four had, in the last year, lived together. Six younger members of the Hardt family had emigrated earlier, but their efforts to get the older members out of Germany were unsuccessful. In addition, there were three widows, ranging in age from fifty-four to sixty-nine, whose husbands had died earlier of natural causes. Two of the widows were alone since their children had emigrated, and the third, also alone, had no other family in Sonderburg. There were also two single men: a widower of sixty-four, whose only child had emigrated and who shared lodgings with my grandparents, and old Mr. Miller, aged ninety-four. The group also included a sixty-two-year-old woman who had been mentally ill for many years and was being looked after by one of the widows. Finally, there were my grandparents, both sixty years old.

During the night of July 25, 1942, each of the remaining Jewish homes was visited by an SS officer and the occupants ordered to assemble the following morning at the square in front of the synagogue. They were allowed one small suitcase. At about 7:00 A.M.

the following morning, Irmgard Bilke happened to be at her window when she saw my grandparents emerge from their house and walk quickly "around the corner, they were heading for the synagogue." She called to her parents, "Come quick, look, the Ostermans are going, they have a suitcase." Her mother burst into tears and refused to come to the window while her father hastily pulled down the window shade. Later that morning Frau Tiller saw a furniture van pull up in front of the store in which she worked. "The back door suddenly opened and the van was filled with Jews. I saw Mr. Miller and all the others sitting there quietly. One of the workers from my store ran forward with a blanket, which he placed over old Mr. Miller's knees. I will never forget the look on the old man's face as he courteously thanked the man for the blanket. It was one of the most moving experiences of my life." The final touch of callousness was to force Jews to assemble in front of their own place of worship. All twelve were sent to Theresianstadt and to their eventual deaths.[11] My family received reports many years later from a camp survivor who had known my grandparents there. According to his report, my grandmother died as a result of despair and malnutrition. My grandfather, who had always been a fit and robust man, died only a few weeks later still in fairly good physical health but having given up his will to live.

Thus Sonderburg, a town in which Jews had resided from 1336 to modern times and which had contained families who had lived there for many generations, was finally *Judenrein*—free of Jews.

A street in modern day Sonderburg.

6

SONDERBURG JEWS AND
GENTILES TODAY

Returning to Sonderburg

Today Minna, Martha, Joshua Abraham, members of the Miller family, and others are in their seventies and live in the United States. Forty-five years after the catastrophic events that so altered their lives, the Jewish immigrants express mixed feelings about Germany and their earlier experiences there. Of the nineteen Jewish persons interviewed, plus a few more who were known to me or who were talked about by others, the majority had never returned to Germany and vowed that they would never do so. Their feelings range from a wish to forget to outright hostility: "I'll never set foot on German soil again"; "those bastards, why should I go after what they did to us"; "what for, that's all in the past, I want to forget the whole thing." Those who were most hostile were people who had lost close relatives, primarily parents. In one family, four siblings who had lost their parents had never revisited Germany; all expressed great hostility toward the country, but still showed some respect for the Germany of old, "for what it was like before Hitler." One immigrant who had turned down an offer to emigrate in 1928, preferring the culture and civilization of Germany to his image of American barbarism, declared vehemently that he would never return to "that place" even for a visit, but in the same breath talked at great length and with pride about Germany as the most civilized country in the world, whose achievements in culture and science have never been equaled.

On the other hand, half the people interviewed had returned for either social visits or business reasons. The visitors were those who had had strong friendships with Germans in their youth and wished to meet them and see the country once again. Minna describes a trip to Germany she made only a few years ago:

> I had gone to see my cousin who lives in England. She suggested that we go to Germany, I didn't want to but she talked me into it. We spent time in Frankfurt and she said, let's go to Sonderburg. She went ahead and made arrangements to hire a car and up to the last minute, I didn't want to go. I packed my boots because I remembered the streets of Sonderburg were cobbled. When we arrived, I was sweating. I went to see Christina, my old friend, she greeted me in tears. I met other old friends of mine and they were all so happy to see me. The funniest part was when I was in the hotel, the owner's wife came running out and when she heard I was Minna Helfer, she called out and people came running over. People I didn't even know came up and said, "Hello, let me shake your hand, its so wonderful to see you. You came back and we are so glad to see you." I said I wanted to see Christina who had no telephone and one of them had a car and went to fetch her. Every time we walked through the streets, it was really embarrassing, they all said, "Hello, how are you, do you like it here, hasn't Sonderburg changed for the better?"

After this happy first visit, Minna was invited two years later to a high school reunion party, which seventeen of her old classmates attended. She described it as a wonderful occasion, where she, the only Jew, was treated with friendship and respect, just as in earlier times. The women, all today in their early seventies, spent most of the reunion time reminiscing about their youth and their activities at school. They "laughed a lot," but the intervening period of the 1930s, the Holocaust, and the war were not included in their happy, nostalgic recollections. Since then, Minna has been in correspondence with many of her old friends. Her visits to Sonderburg have ceased, however, as a result of an experience she had there on her most recent trip, in 1982.

She told me the following story shortly after her return home. A woman named Ilse Lehre was born and raised in Sonderburg and emigrated to the United States in 1938. Her mother died a natural death in 1934 and her father was one of the twelve Jews deported in 1942. She was one of the first Jews to begin paying return visits to Sonderburg and apparently visited very regularly in the last twenty years. (When I was doing fieldwork there, I was told by several people that Ilse Lehre had visited often, but since no one there or in the United States knew where she had settled, I was never able to contact her.) She appeared to have a nostalgic pull back to her early roots despite her many years in the United States. About five years ago, she began thinking of settling in Sonderburg again. On a recent visit, she began making efforts to secure accommodation there. One evening she returned to the hotel visibly shaken, saying, "I can't stay here any longer." She explained to one of her friends that "something had happened," but she was unable to talk about it and would write to her later. She left Sonderburg rather abruptly the next morning. A short time later, her American lawyer wrote to Sonderburg authorities to find out if Ilse had, in fact, purchased a property there because he was in the process of settling her estate. Ilse had hanged herself. The hotel owner related this story to Minna in August 1982. The speculation was that someone, or perhaps more than one person, had discouraged Ilse from resettling in Sonderburg and that this may have contributed to her suicide. The hotel owner apparently agreed with the policy of discouraging Jews to resettle in Sonderburg because he commented to Minna that "it's OK if you come to visit for a couple of days, but living here is an entirely different story." The tragedy of Ilse's suicide and its possible causes, as well as the hotel owner's comment, have now convinced Minna that she will never return to visit Sonderburg again, despite the continued invitations from some of her old friends.

Other former residents of Sonderburg have returned for visits. Alice described her return visit as an enjoyable and very moving experience: "The first person I went to see was Mrs. Fuchs, my old boss in the beautician's shop who had trained me. I went to her house and rang the bell. She called out, 'Go away, I don't want to buy anything.' I answered, 'It's me, Alice, Marx's Alice!'* She opened the door and I thought she would have a heart attack. 'Alice, Alice, you've come back to see me.' " Mrs. Fuchs was then in her eighties. She invited Alice in and they had coffee and cake and reminisced about old times. Otto, the old grocer still serving in the family store, described the return of Walter Hardt: "The bell in the store rang and I went out to serve the customer. A man in a gray hat stood there and I said, 'Can I help you?' He looked at me and said, 'Otto, don't you know me. I'm Hardt's Walter,' and he threw his arms around me." Otto and Walter enjoyed a glass of schnapps in the back of the store as they talked of old times.

Aside from the story of Ilse, Sonderburg Jews who have returned for visits all describe the warm welcome that they received from their old Gentile friends and acquaintances. Most experienced what I encountered there, that is, an eagerness to talk nostalgically about the past. Much of their conversation also centered on the progress that people and their children had made in the intervening years. They were warm reunions between people who had grown up together in the same small community and both participants were eager to catch up on the news of what had happened to others they knew. However, except for oblique and euphemistic references, such as "before the terrible times" or "after the terrible times," the Nazi period was not discussed.

One of the most interesting return visits to Sonderburg was that of John Miller, who passed through the area in the spring of 1945 with the American army. John served as an interpreter with the Third Army division in France and later in Germany. While his division rested before attempting to cross the Rhine, he received permission to visit Sonderburg. His account of the experience is worth quoting at some length:

> I was with the Third Army armored division serving as an inter-
> preter. We had come all the way through France and then into
> Germany. In March 1945, we were near Kreuzen and the officer in
> charge said that the following days' objective was Kreuzen. I told
> him I knew Kreuzen well, that I was born only a few miles from
> there. The officer called the commanding colonel and he asked me
> to come over and asked, "How deep is the river there, can we ford
> the river?" I replied, "No, the water is too deep and the hills are

---

*This form of identification, surname first followed by the given name, is typical of this area of Germany and a practice followed by both Jews and Gentiles.

too steep; and so on. Anyway, in one of the little towns, we took some folks prisoner and I asked them: "What happened in Sonderburg? Do you know anyone by the name of Miller?" "Yes," one man answered; "there were some Jews who lived there a few years ago but they are not there anymore." I didn't say who I was!

A few days later the division forded the river by jeep, and John laughingly recalled that the water was not too deep nor were the hills that steep. His story continues:

After we crossed the river, I found some people who had been evacuated from Kreuzen and who had known my family. Then they told me of my uncle's deportation and I began to get the drift of what had happened. I drove on to Sonderburg with another German-speaking interpreter. I get there and first I drove to my uncle's house to find Marie, his housekeeper, but she wasn't there. I drove through town and up Kirchstrasse—I don't even know what it's called now—and I saw her walking by. I waved to her, but I kept on driving and drove up to the building which had been our mill. I noticed that nothing was too disturbed; there was not much fighting here. The Americans just passed through, but there was little enmity toward them here in the Rhineland.

Anyway, I stopped in front of the mill and a little old lady came up and I just looked around and didn't say a word. The other soldier and I were just standing there and she said in German, "Aren't you young Miller, dirty GI?" "Yes, I am, how did you know?" And she said, "Yes, you really are." Then a whole bunch of people came running up—she had mobilized half the town. They came running to shake my hand, asking, "Are you going to stay here now? Are you going to run the town? Are you going to run the mill again?" Then the manager of the mill, the one in charge for the new owners, took me into his office. He cried and then he said, "Stay here now," and I answered, "No, I'm not staying here, I have to go, I am a soldier now."

Later that day, John met the mayor and another town official who wanted to talk to him:

So we all met at somebody's house and we talked. They told me of Mr. E., whose wife had been Jewish, but they were divorced and she went to live in Switzerland. They had been my parents' friends. But everybody was reassuring to me. I drove up to the cemetery and found it a mess. Later I tried to find one of my teachers from the school, but I didn't find him. He was very prominent in the destruction of our house during Kristallnacht. His name was Rattman. I was going to be violent with him, but I didn't have the chance to be.

Then I drove to the house and met my uncle's former housekeeper. She recognized me right away and that was a very emotional visit. Then I went on from there and rejoined my division.

Thus, the first Jew to return to Sonderburg was not only the scion of its former leading Jewish family but also a member of the victorious American army. The irony of his encounters takes on a double meaning. There is more than a hint of a wistful return to the past in the townfolk's questioning: are the Millers going to return and run the town again and, more importantly, the factory and the mill as they did in the past? Yet only a few years earlier, some of these same people, including the town's officials, had been Nazis and had participated in the destruction of the cemetery and even of the Millers' own house. These were also the same people who drew their blinds and looked the other way when John's own uncle was deported to a concentration camp. Yet upon his return, John was accorded a warm and reassuring welcome.

Of the people who returned, about half did so for social purposes. The other half had to return to reclaim lost business and property interests; they went strictly for financial reasons and did not bother to visit old friends. But even those who went for business reasons paid a visit to the Jewish cemetery to view the graves of grandparents and other relatives buried there.

Feelings About Sonderburg, Then and Now

Almost all of the immigrants identified themselves as American. They all spoke English well, although with an accent; their children, most of whom had been born here, were completely American. They are characteristically patriotic, and for them America, despite some of its problems, can do no wrong. Two of the men volunteered for service in the American army in the early 1940s, although they had only recently arrived in the country, and both were disappointed to be rejected because of their age.

With few exceptions, the Jewish survivors believe that all Germans knew everything there was to know about Nazi policy, in particular the planned extermination of the Jews. They do not generally distinguish between voluntary and enforced Nazi party membership; the fact is lost on the Jewish survivors that officials and civil servants, regardless of their feelings, were often coerced into party membership so as to retain their jobs. Some persons paid lip service to this mitigating circumstance. The woman who said "Of course they were forced to join, else they would have lost their jobs, but they were all Nazis anyway" sums up the beliefs of most of the survivors. While condemning all Germans, in the next breath people would say, "Of course, there were some decent Germans too, even in Sonderburg." Or respondents would say, "They were all Nazis, they hated us," and a few minutes later they would describe German acts of kindness to remaining Jewish families. The considerable ambivalence in the minds of Jews today when they consider Nazi Germany is expressed in their stating these two contradictory views almost simultaneously. One feeling unanimously shared by the Jewish survivors is that the German people, even in Sonderburg, all knew about the concentration camps. As one respondent said, "Of course they all knew the Jews were sent to the KZ [concentration camp], it was not public but people whispered among themselves and everybody knew what was going on." When I suggested that, in communities not located in the vicinity of a death camp and with the absence of media information, there might have been whole towns that did not know about the camps, Jewish respondents scoffed and repeatedly said, "Everyone knew." There is an unwillingness to believe that considerable numbers of rank-and-file Germans may not have had this information and may have assumed that the Jews were being sent either to labor camps or to detention centers in Poland.

Of the Jews who do admit that there were some decent, *anständige* Germans, several families interviewed in the United States said that after the war they regularly sent CARE packages to old German friends.* Alice Marx had been friendly with a German couple who lived in Frankfurt and after the war when they, like others, were destitute and often hungry, Alice sent packages on a monthly basis. Her husband jokes that on the first of every month their dining room looked like a grocery store laden with products and cardboard boxes ready for mailing. Today when Alice and her husband visit Germany, they regularly stay as guests of this couple. Several others mentioned that they also sent packages or money to one or two people with whom they had been especially close and who in earlier years had been kind to them. Interestingly enough, several Germans wrote to Jews after the war if, by chance, they knew of their where-

---

*CARE packages were parcels of food and clothing sent to Europe after the war primarily by North Americans.

abouts. Usually these were letters of a very special kind: the help wanted was either to have immigration papers sent to leave Germany and enter the United States, or to provide certificates or affidavits testifying that those making the request were not Nazis. One such case has already been described: Minna's father receiving such a request from the veterinarian who was, in fact, an important Nazi in the community. John Miller's father received several letters from employees in the factory requesting similar help. None of these letters was answered by the Jews who received them—they simply threw them away. Such requests were treated with contempt. As one older woman said, "The nerve of those Nazis asking us, the victims, for help." They were not moved by the sadness of letters, which described the miserable condition of postwar Germany.

Old Mrs. Frankel, the matriarch of the Miller family, is in her late eighties and the oldest Jewish survivor I was able to interview. Her feelings today are mainly nostalgic, and, as we sat in her comfortable living room drinking tea, she told me mainly of the good times in Sonderburg when she grew up there at the turn of the century. She had many friends, Jewish and Gentile, and her school experiences were happy. She remembered with pleasure rowing on the river with friends on a spring Sunday afternoon, admiring the vine grapes as they were beginning to ripen. Her conversation was filled with such nostalgic reminiscences. Suddenly, she got up, pulled a photo album from the bookshelf, and took from it a faded newspaper clipping, which she handed to me. It showed a picture of her and her late husband, smiling, receiving their American citizenship papers in 1946. The accompanying article described their origins and new life in the United States. As Mrs. Frankel talked about the clipping, her soft voice became hard and almost ferocious: "The first thing I did was to buy another copy of the newspaper. I cut out the clipping intending to send it to Germany, but to whom? Then I remembered the town barber and I sent it to him with a short letter saying, 'See, here we are today.' I knew that from the barber it would get all over town and I wanted them to know how well we were doing and that we were *American citizens* and we didn't need them anymore and we would never need them again." She said she reveled in the knowledge that the German people were in misery while she, her husband, and their family had become thriving, prosperous American citizens. This sense of revenge and bitterness was reflected in the harsh tones of her otherwise quiet and gentle voice.

Several cities in Germany have sponsored reunions with their

former Jewish residents as part of the *Wiedergutmachung* (Resti-
tution) policy of the German government. Organizing these reunions involves searching for survivors, usually through German-
Jewish newspapers published in New York or by word-of-mouth
inquiries. They are invited to return to their community for one
week on an all-expenses-paid trip where they are wined, dined, and
welcomed by the local officials. Frankfurt, with its formerly large
Jewish community, sponsors fifty families per year. The town of
Sonderburg has so far not initiated a reunion, but Alice's husband,
who comes from a neighboring town, was invited to a reunion in
the summer of 1981. She and her husband were looking forward to
the visit, but several other Jews said that they would decline such
an invitation. As Martha put it, "They could pay me an extra $10,000
and I wouldn't go. They can keep their *Wiedergutmachung* policy—
they can never pay us for what they did to us."

One significant event that involved the former Jewish community of Sonderburg was the unveiling of a remembrance plaque
in the Jewish cemetery commemorating the Jews who had died in
World War I, as well as the more recent victims of Nazism. This
event took place in 1950 and was attended by the mayor of the town
and other officials, a leading rabbi from Frankfurt, and several
hundred of the town's citizens. The entire event was sponsored by
Mr. Miller, the factory owner who returned to Sonderburg specifically for this ceremony. The afternoon consisted of speeches by the
assembled guests, but it began with Mr. Miller reading the plaque
on which a large mended fissure could still be seen. The plaque,
rescued from the Jewish synagogue, had been partially destroyed
during Kristallnacht. It bore the names of the World War I dead, and
the lower part read, "To the memory of the sisters and brothers of
our community who fell as victims of National Socialism in
1933–45," followed by a list of thirty-one names, which were slowly
read out by Mr. Miller's son. In his speech, which began, "My
friends, so may I well call you," Miller noted that this was a beautiful
part of the world from which they could see the beautiful town of
Sonderburg, where many people lived in friendly togetherness, each
serving his own God. It was difficult for him to grasp that only a
few years before a devil had been let loose there and everywhere in
Germany, but so it was and this memorial was meant to commem-
orate the victims of those times. What is noteworthy in these few
words is that Miller praised the country's beauty and friendliness.
It was as though every attempt was being made to erase or even
excuse the past as an evil aberration in an otherwise virtuous nation.

Though some might well want the past put to rest other speakers, such as the rabbi, noted that from such darkness, "from this story, we should learn how to make . . . [life] better—there is nothing worse than to create illusions." Several other speakers, including the Protestant minister and the Catholic priest, spoke movingly of the necessity for all to live under God's protection. Today, the plaque is read by every returned visitor to the community, and the unveiling ceremony is recalled by many German residents who were present or who read of it in the local newspaper. Herr Tiller, who had a key to the cemetery, took me there and, as we stood in front of the plaque, told me the story of its unveiling and commented quietly, "You see, we have not forgotten our Jews." What this comment fails to note, however, is that the whole event was initiated by a former Jewish resident who, in the very act of forgiveness, called attention to the guilt of the past. The cooperation and participation of town officials in this event served as an implied reminder of their guilt and complicity. Today townspeople speak of it as their own event.

The Miller family, because of its former prominence in the town, maintained ties with Sonderburg and, in fact, reopened the factory there shortly after the war. In addition to sponsoring this event, Mr. Miller decided to donate a parcel of land (1,700 square meters) in the lower end of the town and, in 1951, the mayor announced the gift to the town council. The council expressed its gratitude and decided to transform the land into a park and recreation area named after a recently deceased son of the family. In 1952, properly designed and landscaped, the Arnold Miller Park was officially opened to the public. Some years later, when the Miller factory celebrated its centennial, the town council voted to rename one of the town's streets Millerstrasse, in recognition of the family's influence on the economic development of Sonderburg. In 1966 the then director of the firm was officially presented with a Federal Order of Merit.

Thus, in recent times the name and activities of the town's leading Jewish family have been kept alive in the history of the community. It was clearly important to the senior Mr. Miller that these ties be maintained; for him, as for many Jewish survivors, the identification with Germany and Sonderburg was still an important part of his life, even after the Holocaust, the war, and his prosperous resettlement in the United States. Not everyone in the family agreed with the donation of the land to Sonderburg, however. At least one family member said that it would have been better to do something in the United States, which had become a haven for Jews and afforded them new opportunities, rather than going back in time to offer a donation to the German town. But as she admitted rather wistfully, "Some of us keep on looking backward."

Life in the United States

The negative feelings of many Jews were reinforced by their incredible struggle in reconstructing their lives in the United States. People felt a tremendous sense of relief when they arrived in the United States, a welcome feeling that finally they were safe. They were among the lucky ones. But on the other hand, having to begin all over again in a strange country meant facing severe hardships. Many experienced a loss in status since they took any jobs that they could find. Very few survivors managed to bring any money, although several did bring personal effects such as furniture, china, and silverware. Most people settled in places where they already had relatives—this usually meant New York City, although a few settled elsewhere. The Martin family immediately settled in upstate New York, where their great-uncle lived. The Miller family all migrated to Massachusetts, where their new mill was located. At least four of the younger Sonderburg Jews also settled there because they had been promised jobs by the Millers, having worked for the Millers earlier. Although there was some measure of continuity in their original settlement, none of the four remained, and during the 1940s they moved to New York City to seek different and better paying jobs. In New York the scramble for jobs was difficult. Joshua Abraham, who had been the religious leader and a schoolteacher, worked as a busboy in a cafeteria. His cousin worked as a street cleaner, and his wife cleaned washrooms in a large office building. Several of the families obtained jobs in the clothing industry in New York, where they worked for below union wages, cutting and assembling clothes. One man began his career delivering carts loaded with clothes along the streets to a building where they were packed and sent to shops; his wage was thirty-five cents per hour. A woman began selling odds and ends on the boardwalks and beaches of the city, trudging along in the hot sand with a pack of goods on her back. She then worked for a retail store, still selling on the beaches; she was finally promoted to work in the shop as a salesgirl. Their wages were all low, but since all adult members of a family were employed, the combined income was enough to manage. Given these kinds of jobs, it is no wonder that their bitterness and hostility toward all Germans was reinforced. They had been forced to leave a prosperous life for one filled with financial worries and other kinds of insecurities. These feelings of hostility have been maintained over the intervening years; but it is interesting to note that their hostility did not spread to the Americans who refused to recognize their skills and exploited their labor.

As time went on, most of the immigrants were able to establish themselves with some degree of success and prosperity. Those employed in the clothing trade became union members and advanced in position and salaries. At least two families eventually bought farms and went into the poultry business. Another two opened factories of their own, one manufacturing zippers and another industrial cloth. Members of the one professional family passed exams and began their professional careers in medicine again. The first-generation survivors are today fairly well off, and several families own vacation properties or rent vacation homes every year in Florida. Those who did not leave New York settled in the Washington Heights area of the city, where a German Jewish ghetto, or residential concentration, is still to be found. But several families moved to Long Island and other suburbs, while some moved to the neighboring states of New Jersey and Connecticut. A few moved out to Illinois and Michigan.

Contacts among the Sonderburg Jews have not been extensive. Most people know all the other migrants and are vaguely aware where they live, but a social life with regular contacts has not been maintained, except in the case of a few. Occasionally, word-of-mouth news travels through the groups, primarily announcing the death of one of the immigrants. Almost all the survivors read *Der Aufbau* (Reconstruction), the German-language Jewish newspaper, in which news of marriages, deaths and funerals is routinely published. Most people explain their lack of connections with the others as a result of the early days, when all were so busy trying to make a living and reestablish themselves that they gradually drifted apart. Once people were established, their energies were directed toward their children, and their social lives revolved around the people in their immediate neighborhood, many of whom were German Jews from other areas of the country, and others from East European countries. Apparently, none in the migrating generation established social ties with non-Jews. Among their children, however, there has been a considerable amount of intermarriage with non-Jews.

One of the notable characteristics among Jewish survivors today is their enormous emphasis on money and security. Many talk about how hard they worked and some are still working in their sixties and seventies to amass money. The money is not spent on consumer goods, property, or holidays since the majority of the Jews I visited live in modest apartments or small, five- or six-room, houses. The funds are invested so that there is a comfortable financial cushion to fall back on in case of need. The survivors talk about each other in terms of how much money they have: "Oh, so and so, yes, he's got a lot of money" or "The X family, yes they are very rich—they're rich people again." When I asked if they were saving their money merely to leave a good legacy to their children, people were reticent, until finally Mr. Abraham answered, "Well, you know, in case we need the money again, to get out, or to offer bribes, or to buy papers. . . ." It became clear that many of the survivors felt an underlying fear that they would be chased and forced to flee for their lives again. This from people living comfortably in the United States as American citizens! Their involuntary exile has left them deeply impaired by fear and insecurity, which they believe only money in the bank can allay.

The Feelings of Sonderburg Gentiles Then and Now

The phrase "The destruction of the Jews was the beginning of the end of Germany" sums up the feelings of most Gentiles in the town today. In retrospect, many people think that this act, more than any other, led to the downfall of what was a "beautiful, wonderful country." They claim that the Reich "should have left the Jews alone," that Jews would even have helped in the war effort because they were first and foremost Germans: "The Jews participated in the First World War and died for the Fatherland, they would have done so again; Hitler should have asked the Jews for help." This somewhat naive view ignores the considerable amount of anti-Semitism that existed even before Hitler's time, although most people, including the Jews, maintained that they could live with some degree of anti-Semitism. Massive genocide was another story. The Hitler regime is today thought to have been a complete aberration from traditionally democratic German patterns. Many Germans feel that the Allies would not have been as harsh toward Germans after the war had the horrors of the Holocaust not occurred: "We would have been treated like any other defeated nation after a war; even more than the takeover of Czechoslovakia and Poland, it was what happened to the Jews which did us in."

People today are quite defensive when they speak of wartime; no one admits to having been a Nazi. A few former party members say that they were forced to join the party to protect their civil service jobs, but they stolidly maintain that they were never committed to Nazi ideology. About twelve persons can be singled out as having been true Nazis occupying leadership positions. According to informants today, there are still a number of followers, but the rest of the community stressed they were totally non-Nazi. Most people today say they were silently compliant because they feared the regime. One man says he routinely gave the Hitler salute but "my heart sank every time I did it." Others describe how they were marshaled together to hear Hitler's speeches over the loudspeakers and listened in disbelief and amazement. One man recounts overhearing a simple worker say at one such rally, "Wenn das geht, dann ist die Bibel falsch" (if this is so, then the Bible is false). The same man notes that in his opinion "Die meisten waren nicht mit Herzen dabel" (in their hearts, most people were not with it). They describe movingly their powerlessness, and the German word *machtlos*, recurred over and over in our conversation. People thought of themselves as powerless, poor people who could do nothing to counteract the horrors of the regime: "Wir waren unter dem Netz gefangen" (we were caught under a net). Many persons note that they wanted to help the Jews but that the spy network was everywhere and any chance comment or act would have been overheard and immediately reported. Imprisonment was the normal procedure for anyone reported as speaking against the regime. One man recalls that his neighbor was picked up for questioning because he had pointed to pictures of Bismark, Wilhelm II, and other past German leaders hanging in the vestibule of the *Rathaus* (town hall) and said, "They were better than what is happening today." He asked, "What would have happened if we had helped the Jews when even such a comment meant questioning or imprisonment?" On the other hand, Mr. A., a party member rounded up to destroy Jewish properties during Kristallnacht, refused and went home without any penalty. In fact, very little punishment took place in Sonderburg.

German respondents are also embarrassed and feel that they were duped. "We were made fools of," they say, not only because Germany lost the war but because so many atrocities were committed by their state. Many of the older Germans today feel implicated by the excesses of the regime: "We couldn't say [after the war] we didn't know; no one believed us and we were all treated like dirt because we belonged to the state." Veterans in particular believe that victory was impossible because so much of the German energy was directed against killing the Jews "instead of killing the enemy."

On the subject of concentration and death camps, all the persons interviewed maintained that they did not know of their existence, nor did any one else in their community or others. The only people who might have known were those who lived in the direct vicinity of a camp and could see and smell what was taking place there. Given that most of the notorious camps were outside of Germany, this in effect may mean that very few Germans were cognizant of the existence of such camps. The common belief was that Jews were sent to labor camps as slave laborers to manufacture munitions and other instruments of war. Another commonly held view was that Jews were sent to Poland to a reservation, where they were allowed to live in peace. It was only after the war, when returning soldiers and news media reported the horrors of the camps, that people learned the truth about where the Jews had been sent. They had lived through an almost total blackout on news about domestic events or anything taking place outside of Germany. Most citizens claim that they did not even know that Germany was losing the war because important defeats such as El Alamein and Anzio were not reported by the German media. The regime censored everything. Several of the respondents said that people would banter with those who were doing something wrong or stupid, saying, "Hör auf, oder du gehst ins KZ" (stop that, or you'll go to a concentration camp), "Ab nach Dachau" (off to Dachau), or "Halts Maul, sie nehmen dich nach Dachau" (shut up, they will take you to Dachau). The Jewish respondents unanimously disagreed with such sentiments. They all believed that ordinary Germans did know and asked, "How could they not?" One man noted that his great-aunt used to whisper about camps where Jews were tortured and killed and she tried to urge her family to leave the country quickly. She was nicknamed the "Horror-story Aunt," since her stories were taken as sensationalized and listeners did not want to believe her. Several Jewish survivors posed this question: "How did a Jewish woman in the same community come to know about the existence of camps while most Germans did not?"

Did They Know?

Discussion surrounding the German people's ostensible knowledge of the genocide is, in some respects, crucial to understanding how surviving Jews perceive their old Gentile friends even today. Jewish survivors are convinced that all Germans had this knowledge, but they may have become more certain of it with the passage of time and the evidence supplied by the war trials in 1945. However, even the high-ranking Nazis on trial said that "one should not believe anyone claiming that he knew nothing,"[1] despite the fact that the internal correspondence among the security police, SS party leaders, and other officials was full of euphemisms such as "resettled" and "evacuated" when referring to the Jews. Sonderburgers claim that what little news they received was carefully filtered. The words "killed," "destroyed," "annihilated" are never mentioned in conversation today. The question remains even today: where did Germans think Jews were being deported and for what purposes? At best people will say, "It's only later that we knew what happened to them."

L. Stokes notes that "just as Nazi social policy, for example, was very different in 1933 from what it became in 1939, so too the regime's racial program underwent a steady evolution after 1933, almost invariably in the direction of increasing radicalization. . . . What is required is greater precision in relating probable knowledge to specific events."[2] Thus, from 1933 to 1939, well-publicized developments came about, such as discriminatory legal measures, attacks on property, the Nuremberg race laws, the Kristallnacht destruction, and eventually the creation of concentration camps. Germans were clearly witness to these occurrences and Stokes notes that "it seems fair to conclude that prior to September 1939 the German people were thoroughly aware of the repressions and persecution of their Jewish fellow citizens, that they generally accepted the government's anti-Jewish measures when these were legally enacted and more or less quietly applied; and that many of them displayed shock and disapproval at a public exhibition of violence towards the Jews."

This conclusion would certainly summarize the feelings and reactions of the Sonderburg German population. As for concentration camps, Stokes argues that the best known were on German soil and near major urban centers; they included Dachau (Munich), Buchenwald (Weimar), and Sachsenhausen (Berlin). Of these, Dachau was best known in Sonderburg since it too was located in southern Germany. Up to 1940 the majority of the camps' inmates were German and Austrian political prisoners, in addition to some Jews. Some inmates were regularly released under an oath of secrecy as to their experiences there, but their release "Insured that the terror function that the KZ's were designed to help exercise was widely known."³

John Miller, a soldier in the American army, participated in the liberation of a small camp in Germany. He talked to some of the surviving inmates, including two young men who still looked fairly healthy, having worked in the kitchen. They said that when they were marched through the town, people would throw stones and spit at them. They sometimes got meat for the camp because the butcher was a communist and would even give them some extra meat for themselves. This same soldier, with the help of his superior officers, organized truckloads of Germans to be driven through the camp so that they could see the atrocities firsthand. (The American colonel refused to let women be mobilized for the tour because he considered the sight too horrible for their exposure.)

During the war the regime was able to put into practice its Final Solution of genocide against the Jews. Most of it was carried out in Poland and later Russia, but despite the distances, reports began filtering back to the German population. Deportations were officially described as "emigration" to rural settlements in the east, which is how the majority of Sonderburgers chose to view the situation. Perhaps most Germans did not know the fate of the Jews in exact detail, but it "was out of the question to hide from an often shocked and outraged populace the beatings, suicides, and forced marches through the streets, even when the operation was carried out as often as possible in the very early hours of the morning." In Sonderburg, several people witnessed the removal of twelve Jews. They described to me their shock and horror at seeing the furniture van filled with elderly Jews awaiting deportation. No one, of course, did anything about it, but news of the event was quickly spread by word of mouth to the entire community. Here, as elsewhere in Germany, "It is difficult to escape the conclusion that there was scarcely another country whose population accepted the carrying away of its Jewish fellow citizens with so little opposition."⁴

In the early 1940s the regime constructed camps in Poland and elsewhere, complete with crematoriums, gas ovens and other accouterments of extermination. Sonderburgers maintained that they did not know about this phase of the program against Jews, but they certainly did know that the earlier political camps existed. Information about the death camps was probably available even in this small community, but few wanted to hear about these atrocities.

Although the Gentiles all insisted with great sincerity that they knew nothing of the extermination camps, and the surviving Jews insisted on quite the opposite, the truth probably lies somewhere in between these two positions. There are several levels of knowing, and undoubtedly many Germans did hear about the camps but closed their minds to what they did not want to know. Jews, of course, would have paid close attention to rumors, whereas German civilians probably dismissed and even repressed such knowledge from their conscious thoughts, especially when they had had good relations with Jewish neighbors and friends. They would not have wanted to believe that people with whom they had grown up and gone to school were being sent to torturous deaths and gas chambers. Perhaps, then, they knew on a certain level but refused to believe and quickly cast the matter out of their minds.

Today many Germans do not want to remember the past and say, "Today, we don't look at those things anymore. We don't ask questions about who was in the party. We have to forget all those things, those terrible times. Life goes on." The irony is that they all do remember who were party members and who were Nazis. This much is clear from the impassioned recollections of these old people, now mostly in their seventies and eighties; they have not forgotten and will never forget.

Probably for the last thirty years, many Gentile Germans have felt sorrowful about all the destruction the war caused. The thrust of their feelings, however, is not so much toward the fate of the Jews but toward what they themselves endured during and after the war. My conversation with German respondents can be broken down into three segments or stages. First, they would express sorrow and sadness about the Jews, then they would discuss their own sufferings during and immediately after the war, and, finally, they would note that conflicts and wars are still evident in the world today, saying, "People are always being bad—that is human nature." After emphasizing their powerlessness to help the Jews, they would return to their own suffering, telling stories of their near-starvation due to food shortages and their inability to buy goods, despite occasional barters with farmers who still had produce. The women especially mourned the loss of their husbands and sons to the war effort. They expressed an enormous amount of hostility toward the Allies, particularly the Russians and the Americans, for bombing Germany, destroying the country, and killing innocent women and children. They were apparently unaware that Hitler himself planned the total destruction of the country during the very last days of the war, and they expressed much less hostility toward their former

Nazi regime. They seldom mentioned the fact that Hitler began the war and was directly responsible for its aftermath.

The Americans were particularly faulted for denying citizens food or for sending them spoiled food, "as though we were animals." Frau Tiller, for example, told me in bitter tones how she used a small needle to pick out the bugs from each lentil seed that Americans had sent them. Her husband added that, on one occasion, she failed to find all the bugs and he discovered some insects on his dinner plate. He has never been able to eat lentils since. According to his wife, "we were just innocent people and they made us starve." Stories of privation were legion. Townspeople scouted the countryside attempting to barter farm products for household articles, and as one man noted, "farmers lined the floors of their stables with Persian carpets." The demolished buildings, rubble on the streets, and bombed out craters were all secondary to the lack of food. Several persons realized that German prisoners of war were being treated even worse and they often told of a nearby prisoner-of-war camp, where 40,000 prisoners were left to die of malnutrition. One survivor of that camp reminded me, however, that prisoners of war were treated according to international rules and not left to starve. But stories of horror and atrocity committed by the Allies were more often recounted than those about concentration camps. Several Sonderburgers had to evacuate their homes and stay with friends when the town was occupied by Allied troops passing through the area. Frau Mauer recalled that her family had troops quartered in its house for a period of three weeks and they "never cleaned the bathtub and they played popular songs on my grand piano," but she went on to say that their presence was only a minor irritation compared to "what happened to our beautiful Fatherland." Her husband quickly interrupted (perhaps for my benefit) and said, "But remember, Marie, it was our Fatherland that started it all—if only we had not had Hitler, the maniac, at the helm." On the whole, men were more objective than women in describing those times. Women were more in touch with the realities of lost sons and the need to find scanty provisions for their remaining families, and they vented their anger on the Allies who, in their eyes, created such unfair and intolerable conditions for innocent Germans. They also recalled that among their worst experiences was listening to the nightly bomb raids. Sonderburg was only slightly bombed, but a nearby munitions plant was completely destroyed. Some of the town's men missed those events, having spent the war on the Russian front and elsewhere.

For the German people in Sonderburg, their own frightful war and postwar experiences took precedence over the Jewish problem, as is perhaps to be expected. Besides, if indeed they learned about the fate of the Jews only after the war, then this discovery coincided with the height of their own suffering. The third phase of the discussion usually involved armed conflict in the world today. The Iran-Iraq war, or the earlier Vietnam and Korean wars were pointed out as examples of human nature at its aggressive worst. Their implicit point was that they were not that bad, that others are equally bad and that there is war now just as there has been throughout human history. They argued, "We Germans are not the only guilty ones," and, in any case, "We were the innocent and duped victims of a regime—we were the little people."

W. Laqueur notes that although the numbers directly involved in the Final Solution were small, this program couldn't have been carried out without the help or knowledge of a great number of people. He points in particular to the important role of the railway in transporting Jews to the death camps. Railway cars were directly commissioned by the SS, and a large staff was involved in their running and maintenance. The incineration of Auschwitz was done less than a mile away from the railway station and, although Sonderburg is nowhere near Silesia, the death camp's location, it is still quite probable that word filtered even to this relatively isolated town. Laqueur indicates that even though very few people had detailed information, hundreds of thousands must have learned something about the Jews' fate from officers and soldiers returning to their communities on leave.[5] Several German soldiers returned to Sonderburg on leave. Today none of the old people will describe what they heard, but it is all too likely that those returning soldiers brought reports of the massive killings of the Jews.

In one community almost as small as Sonderburg, a returned soldier had written a letter to the press describing the killing of Jews in southern Ukraine—letters from Germans stationed in the east were apparently not censored. Herr Tiller served on the eastern front and among his many horrible recollections were stories of the annihilation of Soviet and Jewish citizens in 1944. He described how he saw a "truckload" of people, Jews and Russians, taken into a warehouse, how the doors and windows were locked and then the truck exhaust was piped in and all died of carbon monoxide poisoning. He also saw "a concentration camp filled with dying people." In his book *German and Jew: The Life and Death of Sigmund Stein*, Dickinson quotes an official in Hochberg who was "aware of rumors about 'actions' which had occurred in the wake of the German advance into Russia: 'Soldiers on leave from SS units would either tell stories to their wives under the seal of domestic confidence or make obscure allusions to such actions elsewhere. The matter would then get around slowly, as confidence about confidence' "[6] It is quite probable that Tiller mentioned these events to his wife and family in his letters. Even in small Sonderburg many of the people must have had an inkling of what was being done to the Jews although their information may not have been elaborate. But it should be remembered that times were hard in small German towns during the war. Food shortages, the drafting of men by the military, and the fear already evident in 1942 that Germany was losing the war meant that the population was living under severely threatening conditions. Because of the general fear and suspicion that surrounded their lives, few people probably gave more than a passing thought to the fate of the Jews.[7] Trying to survive under a repressive regime was the uppermost concern for the Gentile population; as Herr Maurer said, "Even if we had known about the death camps, what could we have done about them?" W. Laqueur corroborates these views:

> Millions of Germans knew by late 1942 that the Jews had disappeared. Rumors about this fate reached Germany mainly through officers and soldier returning from the Eastern front but also through other channels. There were clear indications in the wartime speeches of the Nazi leaders that something more drastic than resettlement had happened. . . . Quite likely that while many Germans thought that the Jews were no longer alive, they did not necessarily believe that they were dead. Such belief . . . is logically inconsistent, but a great many logical inconsistencies are accepted in war time.

The fate of the Jews "was an unpleasant topic, speculation was unprofitable, discussions of the fate of the Jews were discouraged. Consideration of this question was pushed aside, blotted out for the duration."[8]

The evidence suggests that, even in a small town, some information about the Final Solution was surely known, though this should be understood within the wider international context. Information on the extermination of Jews was disseminated to Britain, the United States, Palestine and elsewhere. It was not believed by foreign authorities, and even Jewish leaders were slow to accept these reports. They were too accustomed to the usual pogroms that

East European Jewry had been subjected to over the centuries; they thought this another pogrom perhaps, or even a segregation into labor camps, but could not believe that total annihilation was possible. Jewish leaders abroad totally misjudged the extent of Nazi vindictiveness against the Jews. It should also be remembered that many Jews themselves could not believe even as late as 1938 or 1939 the extent of the horrors being inflicted on their people, and the Final Solution was not believed by Jews in Europe even as late as 1942. The content of reports smuggled out of Switzerland and into the United States was, at the behest of American Jewish leaders themselves, kept from general public knowledge, presumably because of doubts about its veracity. Thus the extent of the Final Solution was not known to American Jews until the mid-forties. Finally, it has now become clear that no government—American, British, Russian, or any other—had any real interest in the fate of European Jews.[9]

The author's grandparents and their children in 1928; a prosperous middle class Jewish family just a few years before history was to change their lives.

7

AN ANALYSIS OF INTERETHNIC RELATIONS IN SONDERBURG

Thus far I have been describing relations between Jews and Gentiles in Sonderburg. In this chapter, I propose to analyze these relations in a more systematic manner using some of the theoretical propositions and insights offered by social anthropologists and sociologists who have been examining ethnic relations and the whole issue of ethnicity for many years. I have been guided in the discussion that follows by the works of M. Gordon, R. A. Schermerhorn, M. G. Smith, and others, and in particular by the seminal work of Frederick Barth.[1]

In the growing field of ethnicity studies, theorists have mainly concentrated on the process of assimilation. Among the sociologists spearheading these studies, M. Gordon put forth the premise that ethnic groups, especially in the United States, were moving toward assimilation. However, more recent work in the United States indicates that aspects of ethnicity remain or reemerge in the third generation. Consequently, the emphasis in studying ethnicity has shifted to analyzing the process of integration. What has also stirred interest is the question of the so-called boundary-maintaining mechanisms between ethnic groups—how ethnic groups maintain their distinctiveness and in what ways they are seen as distinct by other groups.

With regard to Sonderburg, it becomes quite clear that some aspects of ethnicity are more relevant than others. Barth's concept of boundary maintenance is particularly useful for this case study since Jews and Gentiles in Sonderburg did observe clear-cut social boundaries, although they reconciled their differences and lived together without overt conflict. M. Gordon's distinction between cultural and structural integration also applies to the situation. (Cultural integration refers to the ways in which two or more groups share and believe in the same value system whereas structural integration involves the extent to which a group, usually a smaller or weaker one, is able to gain access to the institutions of society. For example, are they able to participate fully in the occupational structure? attend the same schools as the more dominant group? participate in the political arenas? etc.) On the other hand, the concept of assimilation, though often used to describe the position of Jews in Germany, does not help in analyzing ethnic relations within Germany in general or Sonderburg in particular. Sonderburg Jews were not totally assimilated into the mainstream of town life; in fact, it is extremely doubtful that Jews were ever totally assimilated anywhere in Germany. To discuss their status in these terms merely adds to the confusion already existing in some of the literature.[2] Looking at integration and the mechanisms that maintain boundaries helps clarify the ethnic situation in Germany and in the small town of Sonderburg.

Since most Jews completely accepted and believed in mainstream German values—often referred to as *Deutschtum*—it is plain that they achieved a considerable amount of cultural integration. As for structural integration, or the degree to which Jews had access to and took part in important institutions, probably it too had occurred to a very considerable degree. If we consider only one aspect of structural integration, namely, access to high-status professions and other occupations, which are important in forming public and media opinion, we find that Jews were vastly overrepresented, as the following table indicates.

Jews were active retailers in business and commerce. Between 1928 and 1932, "Jews represented 25% of all individuals employed

TABLE 1

**Professions in which Jews represented more than 5% of those employed,
i.e., more than six times their percentage in the labor force.**

	%
Lawyers and notaries	16.15
Brokers and agents	15.05
Solicitors	13.28
Doctors	10.88
Commercial representatives	9.20
Dentists	8.59
Estate managers	8.53
Furriers	6.33
Directors and stage managers	5.61
Legal consultants	5.40
Editors and publicists	5.05

Source: *Statistik des Deutschen Reiches*, v. 451.

in retail business and handled 25% of the total sales although they represented only .74% of the labour force." Jews also participated in the private-banking sector; in Berlin alone there were 150 private Jewish banks as compared to 11 private banks not owned by Jews. Although Jews also occupied important positions in the non-Jewish banks out of proportion to their numbers in the labor force, they "controlled only a small percentage of all banks in Germany."[3] Jews were also involved in the stock market, the insurance industry, and other financial arenas. Jews were even slightly overrepresented in the civil service and in leading white-collar positions.

In the pedagogic sphere, Jews were overrepresented among university students. German universities accepted Jews on an equal basis with non-Jews as early as 1870. As late as 1929, 4 percent of all university students were Jewish although they represented less than 1 percent of the population. Of course, the large number of university-educated Jews led directly to their overrepresentation in the professions and the arts. This factor also influenced their higher income levels and resulted in the majority of Jews attaining middle-class status. While Jews were overrepresented in certain fields of activity, their comparatively small numbers in the total population and labor force meant that they never dominated any of these fields, nor were Jewish enterprises "the mainstays of national economic strength. Jews were never the powerful 'captains of industry' who produced the bulk of Germany's manufactured goods; rather their role was predominantly that of middlemen."[4]

Jews also participated actively in politics. Around the turn of the century, 2.2 percent of all delegates to the Reichstag or Parliament were Jewish. Later, during the period of the Weimar Republic, this figure rose to 2.8 percent.[5] Many Jews were also active in local politics. Jewish politicians were invariably associated with left-wing parties, particularly the Social Democratic party.

Another indicator of structural integration was the number of Jews who converted to Protestantism. Almost 17,000 adult conversions took place between 1881 and 1933, and, overall, approximately 10 percent of German Jewry left Judaism either to convert or to remain without religious affiliation. A very large proportion of Jews also married outside the faith, although in some instances non-Jewish women converted to Judaism when entering into marriage with Jewish men. As late as 1933, 44 percent of all Jews who married chose partners of a different religion. A significant number of children from mixed marriages were not socialized as Jews; estimates suggest that no more than 25 percent of such offspring were raised as Jews.[6]

Thus, several indices of structural integration suggest that German Jews had made very significant inroads in attempting to integrate with mainstream German society. Some German Jews, particularly those who had converted to Christianity, defined themselves as totally assimilated (yet even these individuals did not escape their Jewish past under Nazism). The majority of "assimilated" Jews lived in the larger urban areas. Yet true assimilation did not take place because Jews maintained their ethnic distinctiveness and were perceived as distinct by Gentiles.

Consider, for example, the account of three fairly "assimilated" Jewish survivors: "We were a very assimilated Jewish family... I studied Hebrew, the Old Testament, and the history of the Jews. But I had no strong feeling for it. My awareness of being Jewish came when the tennis club was restricted. I joined a Jewish club because there was no other way I could get to play.'"[7] This account came from a woman who was born in an urban area and whose nationalistic father was an officer in the Prussian army. Despite her lack of strong feeling for Judaism, its religion and history had been part of her education and she had experienced discrimination on the basis of being Jewish. A man born and raised in Frankfurt's large Jewish community recalled that "Growing up in Frankfurt, if you were a Jew, you were bound to have strong feelings of identity, because your whole world was Jewish.... This was the Germany of the Weimar Republic and we were free to come and go before

Hitler took over, but we definitely lived in a Jewish world." Another survivor from Berlin noted that his family was completely assimilated: "I grew up without knowing I was Jewish, with no Jewish religion, no Jewish instruction, no Jewish cultural interests." This account concluded, however, with a most revealing statement: "Many, if not most, of our friends were Jewish." But the explanation was offered in terms of economics: "Separations between people depended on economics rather than religion."[8] Were there then no Gentiles of a similar economic status with whom this family could have associated?

In analyzing patterns of assimilation or integration among the Jews in Germany, it should also be noted that about one-fifth of them were of East European origin. This group not only adhered to the tenets of religious orthodoxy but it was also far less structurally and culturally integrated with mainstream German society than the remaining four-fifths.

In rural Germany and small towns like Sonderburg, Jews had also achieved a considerable degree of structural integration, particularly in employment, but, as noted in Chapter 1, Jews were economically niched into a few occupational categories. In their earlier history, only money lending was open to them; gradually they entered other low status jobs such as cattle and horse trading, as well as peddling. Over the years, as laws changed, Jews gained greater access to occupations, and from peddling it was a small step to retail merchandising. Once they were allowed to own land, agricultural pursuits also became possible. By the turn of the century, most rural Jews were retail merchants, cattle and horse traders, and small-scale farmers, with a few who had become industrialists. These occupations were virtually guaranteed to give most Jews a fairly comfortable middle-class status. Their structural integration cannot be considered complete, however, because they were strongly concentrated in a few occupations and their access to others, such as the civil service, skilled manual trades, and even the professions, was less than total. It can be argued, though, that the lack of participation in other occupations on the part of rural Jews had something to do with the forces of custom and tradition that were maintained within the community, rather than with discriminatory employment practices.

The Jews' social integration, as described in Chapter 6, was also not complete since even before Hitler's time they faced many closed doors. In Sonderburg, Jews were excluded from social and athletic clubs and other aspects of the town's social life. The very low rate of intermarriage in rural communities also suggests that while friendships and dating relationships between the two groups were possible, total integration in terms of intermarriage rarely occurred.

In sum, then, urban Jews were culturally and structurally integrated with mainstream German society to a far greater extent than were their rural counterparts. In rural communities, patterns of ethnic distinctiveness were maintained through a variety of fairly clear-cut strategies. Barth, in the celebrated essay that introduces *Ethnic Groups and Boundaries*, placed much emphasis on the socially relevant factors involved in ethnic relations, including the importance of a group's self-definition of ethnicity, the perception of nongroup members, and the ways in which ethnic group differences are maintained. These and other ideas of Barth have particular relevance to the Jewish-Gentile interaction in Sonderburg and serve to explain the relationships that existed between these two groups both before and after Hitler.

Interethnic Relationships

Barth and others note that an ethnic group has traditionally been thought to have the following characteristics:

1. It is biologically self-perpetuating.
2. It shares fundamental cultural values.
3. It makes up a field of communication and interaction.
4. It has a membership which identifies itself and is identified by others as a distinguishable category.

Jews in Germany, and specifically in Sonderburg, certainly constituted an ethnic group or category by this definition. Jews by and large maintained a pattern of endogamous, or in-group, marriage and thus maintained themselves biologically, although in urban German society the rates of intermarriage were high. In small towns, however, Jews clearly interacted and communicated among themselves, identified themselves as Jewish, and were so perceived by most Gentiles.

As for the sharing of fundamental values, some clarification is needed. While Jews in Sonderburg did share certain values that distinguished them from non-Jews, most of their other values, beliefs, and goals were quite similar to those of their Gentile neighbors (see pages 160–164). If an ethnic group is distinguishable by its separate value system, then the point must be stressed that German Jews and Gentiles did not fundamentally disagree in their cultural value systems. If Gentiles and Jews shared the same cultural values, then what distinctions served as boundary markers between the two groups?

To summarize the reasons, in the first instance, Jews in Sonderburg maintained their Jewish ethnic identity by in-group marriage (see Chapter 2). Unlike the more urban areas of Germany, Sonderburg and other small communities had low rates of intermarriage. Proscriptions against intermarriage included traditional opposition of Jewish families to their children marrying non-Jews and latent anti-Semitism on the part of some Gentiles. As part of their accommodation to each other, both groups accepted the view that marriage patterns should remain endogamous.

Second, Jews maintained their ties to the religion of Judaism, although those in Sonderburg and elsewhere accepted the tenets of a modified liberal Judaism. Thus, while they were not Orthodox, they did build a synagogue, where weekly services were conducted and attended on a somewhat sporadic basis by most resident Jews. High Holidays and important festivals during the year were observed, as was the traditional rite of passage, the bar mitzvah ceremony for boys thirteen years of age. In addition, the community supported a religious teacher to provide instruction to Jewish youths. Jews also had their own cemetery, but his was the result of former legal interdictions against Jews burying their dead in Christian cemeteries (although at least two Jews had requested permission to be buried in non-Jewish cemeteries earlier in this century). Some culinary traditions such as the baking of challah and the Passover matzoth were continued, as was the customary Friday night meal for family members (to which Gentile friends were occasionally invited).

Third, Jews were fairly specialized occupationally in the commercial sectors of the local economy, primarily as retail merchants and animal traders. This occupational concentration was also a carry-over from earlier times, when trade and commerce were the only occupations that Jews were allowed to enter. In urban areas Jews had made great inroads into the professional and cultural sectors, but in smaller communities they were still concentrated in traditional occupations.

Finally, even the very integrated families retained a sense of Jewishness, "a sense of being different—one always knew there was something different about being Jewish," as one informant put it. Jews clearly defined themselves as Jewish even if, in some youngsters' minds, this meant only a vague sense of being different. Particularly in small towns such as Sonderburg, all the Jews were known and identified as Jews. With respect to language or institutional dimensions, such as political affiliations and commitments, there were no major differences between the two groups. The Jewish community's self-defined boundaries had to do with marriage, family, religion, some degree of occupational concentration and, most crucially, a sense of Jewish identity.

To a certain extent, Jewish boundaries were also maintained by Gentiles, whose perceptions of Jews helped to create and perpetuate ethnic boundaries. Chief among these factors was a degree of anti-Semitism that existed even in this relatively stable community. Earlier legal discrimination had been removed by the middle of the nineteenth century so that direct proscriptions against Jewish ownership of land, employment, and other rights no longer applied, but anti-Semitic attitudes remained in German society. In Sonderburg, discrimination surfaced primarily in the exclusion of Jews from clubs and important social rituals, as well as in the occasional name-calling incidents in school. Some Gentile families also resisted intermarriage with Jews, and at least three known families expressed a virulent hostility toward Jews. While they were not legally or officially excluded from certain occupations, the consensus in the Gentile community was that Jews were expected to be shopkeepers and merchants. Though the Miller factory was viewed as an exceptional case, it did have very humble beginnings in one woman's cottage industry of hand-knitting hosiery at home.

Another subtle form of anti-Semitism was the labeling of Jews and Jewish houses. People would, for example, refer to "the Jew Blau" or "what was the name of that Jewish house on Kirchstrasse." The label "Jew" was used as part of the identification of people and their houses. The idea that Jews were crooked came about because many Jews were animal traders, and since according to popular perception, animal traders were almost always crooks, ergo Jews were crooks. Among the several Jewish animal-trading families in Sonderburg, one was definitely thought to be crooked and was spoken of thus: "Mr. S. would put pepper in a horse's rear end so that it would appear sprightly." However, another family of animal traders was always thought to be honest and fair-dealing.

With respect to language, both Jews and Gentiles spoke a strong Rhineland or, more specifically, River Valley, dialect among themselves and a more standard German on formal occasions. Jews and Gentiles conversed in dialect with each other, as well as among themselves.

While Gentiles did not label each other as Christians, Jews were frequently labeled as Jews. When a Jew traveled outside the community, his or her identity was not readily perceived because such features as style of dress or speech pattern did not distinguish a Jew from anyone else. My Jewish respondents recalled many instances when they passed for Gentiles, and some ironically took place even in Hitler's times. One young woman, who fled from Sonderburg to Hamburg to board a ship bound for England, described how on each train she was courteously helped with her luggage by German passengers, one of whom was a Nazi in full SS regalia, who even politely tipped his cap to her. There were a number of incidents when Sonderburgers traveled to other cities where they were not known among the Gentiles. Minna described a "silly" yet very frightening experience which happened to her in 1938. She was riding the train to nearby Kreuzen "when a Nazi youth group came in and said, of course, 'Heil Hitler.' I didn't say anything. They passed by. I was sitting alone and one of them came back to me and said, 'We have a boy here who is not married and we are going to marry him to you.' I looked at him, he was serious. 'We are twenty here in this compartment and you are the only girl.' I was so scared. He brought a German flag and told us to 'stand up' and then he said, 'I now pronounce you man and wife, Heil Hitler.' " This inability to identify Jews inadvertently helped Jews in the mid- and late 1930s, when they were by law unable to buy in shops. Some made their purchases in other communities where they would not be recognized. Martha sometimes walked to the neighboring village of Stattheim "when we were out of sugar or salt; it was only two and a half kilometers, even as a child it was not far. They didn't know I was Jewish."

Jews who went to other towns to study were known as Jews only if they chose to identify themselves as such. Often even their names could as well be German as Jewish. Many German Jews have names that are not particularly associated with Jewishness, unlike Jews from Eastern Europe, where Cohen, Goldberg, Ginzberg, and the like are known to be Jewish names. My own family name of Osterman is German rather than Jewish and there are more non-Jewish than Jewish Ostermans in both Germany and the United States. Many Jews' physical appearance is also indistinguishable from that of many Germans. Despite Hitler's attempt to redefine the Aryan race, most Germans are dark-haired and dark-eyed, particularly in southern Germany and the Rhineland. One of my respondents laughed as she recalled the Nazis' attempt to portray the Jew as a hawk-nosed, bearded person when all the Jews of her acquaintance "looked just like everybody else." Jews did not have any readily visible characteristics and could easily pass for Gentiles if they chose to do so. In fact, the ease with which they could lose their ethnic identity reinforced their drive toward assimilation into the wider German society.

Thus both groups shared and participated in some of society's institutions, but they nevertheless maintained systematic boundaries around them so that their own distinctive ethnicity could be maintained.[9] Although Protestants and Catholics were not always clearly demarked, everyone always knew who was Jewish.

In summarizing the various institutional affiliations of Gentiles and Jews in Sonderburg, there are only two areas in which major differentiation appeared. In the occupational sphere, as we have seen, Jews were niched into retail trade, whereas Gentiles occupied civil service positions and dominated the municipal structure. Professionals such as lawyers, doctors, accountants, and others were almost exclusively Gentile in this small community. (In larger urban areas, however, many Jews occupied these professional positions.) This occupational differentiation resulted in mutual interdependence. Gentiles relied on Jewish merchants and traders for their purchases and on the Jewish factory for employment, whereas Jews used the services of Gentile professionals and had to deal with them in their administrative capacities. Skilled workers such as plumbers and electricians were also mostly Gentile.

This occupational differentiation led to two separate but occasionally overlapping systems of stratification. The small Jewish sector was heavily middle class, with a three-family elite and an equally small (three to four families) lower class. These groups were created primarily by discrepancies in income, since the three elite families were usually described as *sehr reiche Leute* (very rich people) and the few families below the middle-class group as *arme Juden* (poor Jews). Among the Jews, there was a clear-cut division between the elite Jews and the non-elite. They did not socialize together, and even today middle-class Jews, when referring to the elites, would say that "they had nothing to do with us" or "we were not in their class." However, all Jews, regardless of their class status, shared the same religious facilities and paid for and used the services of the same Jewish religious teacher. They also sent their children to the same public schools for the early grades, and just a few of the older rich children were sent to other areas of Germany or abroad to boarding schools.

Whereas the small Jewish community was predominantly middle class, the very much larger Gentile community was primarily lower or working class. There was a very tiny Gentile elite consisting of three to four families, a moderate middle class of about 300 families and the remainder was working class, mostly made up of wage workers. The Gentile middle class provided the civil servants and professionals, and the few elites were very rich businessmen. In contrast to the majority of the working class, who were Roman Catholic, the majority of the middle- and upper-class Gentiles were Protestant. Between Jews and Gentiles, a moderate amount of interaction took place between the elites, chiefly in the work place and on specified social occasions, such as fund-raising events for charity. As we have already seen, however, the Jewish elite was excluded from the town's most prestigious social club. Most social interaction between the two groups involved the middle class. Jewish and Gentile children from this social level went to school together while their mothers sometimes visited each other for afternoon tea. Middle-class men from both ethnic groups drank and played cards together at the local hotel and cafes. Most of the school and neighborhood friendships described earlier evolved between those in the middle class of the stratification system. For some social occasions, then, common class status was a more salient distinction than ethnic affiliation.

Though both groups sent their children to the local school, they provided separate religious instruction for these children. In politics, local municipal officials were either appointed or elected, depending on their positions. Several elite Jews had held political office around the turn of the century. In the Miller family, both maternal and paternal grandfathers had been in the town council and, earlier, one of their great-grandfathers had also served as a councilor. In another elite family, Mrs. Frankel's father around the turn of the century became head of the town council and could serve as mayor in the mayor's absence. In more recent times, Mr. Miller, the factory owner, was an elected member of the council and was even re-elected, after Hitler had come to power, in the last democratic election held in Germany in 1933. With respect to political party preferences, ethnicity did not appear to differentiate the two groups until the early 1930s, when Jews did not vote for the National Socialists but over 50 percent of their Gentile neighbors did. Communism was little known in this small town, but at least one Jew was said to be a member of the Communist party.

One of the most obvious boundary markers between ethnic groups is the creation and maintenance of residential ghettos, or residential concentrations. In small communities like Sonderburg, residential segregation would have been impossible to maintain even if it had been desired. The small size of the elites in both groups also meant that class segregation was not especially evident. Although there was a poorer section of town centering on one or two streets where both the few poor Jews and the many more poor Gentiles lived, there was no clearly defined rich area. The rich elite in both groups did, however, live in large, detached houses surrounded by substantial gardens, whereas the middle class of both groups tended to live in attached or row houses. The size of house, then, signaled elite status more decidedly than did place of residence. The Jews did not develop an area of the town as their own, and Jewish homes were scattered throughout the community. There was some slight concentration of Jews along both sides of Grossestrasse (Main Street), which was the main business street in the town. Jewish businesses and residences were usually combined in one house.

In addition to occupational differences, the other most significant institutional difference between the two groups was that of religion. But even here, on occasion, special Gentile friends would sometimes be invited to synagogue services. Similarly, Jewish children would sometimes attend an Easter or Christmas service in the company of their Gentile friends.

A difference linked to religion involved membership in organizations that transcended the local community network. One of the most important was the Gemeinde, or corporation—the communal organization based on religion in which all Jews were registered at birth. The Gemeinde was a public body maintained by a system of state taxation to which all Jews contributed. Its function was to maintain synagogues and cemeteries, further religious education, and dispense charity to needy Jews. In Sonderburg, Mr. Abraham's salary as a cantor and religious teacher was paid by the Gemeinde. A committee of elder Jews ran this organization locally, and although the town did not have its own corporation until 1926, Sonderburg belonged to a larger group in a nearby city. Membership in this organization, the appointment of committee members to run the corporation, and the dissemination of its decisions throughout the community all had some significance in differentiating Jews from Gentiles. During the early 1920s, the Jews of Sonderburg worked hard to establish their own corporation. Its creation in 1926 was a major event widely celebrated in the Jewish community.

Another important organization was secular in nature though based on religious affiliation: the Zentralverein deutscher Staatsbürger jüdischen Glaubens (The Central Association of German

Citizens of Jewish Faith). It was established in 1893, in past to foster unity among the Jews, who were deeply divided by doctrinal and regional differences. It also sought to organize German Jewry to withstand the forces of anti-Semitism and, in so doing, paved the way for many other organizations that were formed later to provide cohesiveness to the Jewish sectors of the country. The Zentralverein formed a large pressure group whose aim was to call attention to the fact that "German Jewry had rejected acquiescence or emigration, that instead it had decided to fight for those rights to which it was politically and legally entitled."[10] It campaigned against anti-Semitic political candidates during elections, invoked the judicial system as much as possible, and tried to become an encompassing organization, embracing the entire Jewish population of Germany.

In 1933 the Zentralverein (ZV) had a membership of 70,000, which included 60 percent of all Jewish families. In Sonderburg, there were at least four (and possibly more) residents who were members of the ZV. Two young people joined while going to school in a larger city, and the Jewish teacher and the physician's son were members. Pamphlets and other published material from the ZV were distributed throughout the community so that ZV's activities were known to a large number of Sonderburgers. Since the ZV's primary purpose was to foster Jewishness and act against anti-Semitism, membership or even the reading of its literature was an important feature of Jewish life that was not shared with Gentiles.

Thus far the few institutional differences that existed between Jews and Gentiles were linked to occupation and religion. At the same time, there were numerous institutional similarities: both groups lived together, attended the same educational facilities, participated in the same political structures and shared some, if not all, recreational pursuits. Ethnic distinctiveness was maintained, however, by a pattern of in-group marriage and the Jews' feeling of being different.

Ethnic boundaries are usually perpetuated when two or more groups share some values but also maintain very distinctive and separate value systems. Jews in Germany did not believe that this was the case. Jews shared in and subscribed to essentially the same set of values that characterized German society as a whole. German Jewish intellectuals heralded the total assimilation of the Jews in Germany, and the majority of Jews believed, despite the evidence of past anti-Semitism, that they were utterly and entirely German. Their assumed assimilation set them apart from East European Jews. East European Jews shared a common religion with their German

Jewish counterparts but differed from them in all other behavioral and institutional aspects. They adhered to their own set of values with very minimal participation in those of the wider society. Jews in other European countries were separate from the wider societies in which they lived whereas German Jews were at one with German society and culture. A major Jewish intellectual writing in 1912 came to the conclusion that the differences between German and others Jews were primarily political and national. These problems could be solved by emigration to Palestine, but German Jews were very successful in Germany; they were Germans who "were able to dine with the Kaiser." The view of a number of Jewish writers was that "Jews and Germans had blended together to fulfill the dream of a German nation. Emancipation has facilitated assimilation; and assimilation in turn, had fostered the same pride in all German heroes, German classics, ideals and art in all Germans."[11] These views of assimilation came from the ideas of the Enlightenment, and Jewish idealists saw this as the formative period for German culture. Such values as tolerance, reason, cosmopolitanism, as well as nationalism, understanding, and liberal humanism, were said to characterize German society. As late as the mid-1930s, some Jewish intellectuals dismissed Hitler and his followers as not being in the mainstream of German history, as an aberration from a fixed value system, which therefore could not last. While German Jews were aware of anti-Semitism and its apologists like Chamberlain, Stocker, and later Hitler, they also saw a counterbalance of enlightened figures such as Schiller, Goethe, Kant, and Humboldt. The major Jewish newspaper noted in 1919 that "We are German and want to remain German, and achieve here, in Germany, on German soil, our equal rights, regardless of our Jewish characteristics. . . . Also we want inner regeneration, a renaissance of Judaism, not assimilation."[12] Yet what is acknowledged here is that in all vital respects of values, lifestyle, and intellectual traditions, if "inner regeneration" means only religious or confessional separateness, then assimilation has been accomplished. In Sonderburg too, these attachments to things German were important but sometimes not without conflict. John recalled that "I would hear my parents, even in the 1920s, talk about *deutschvölkish* (or *Deutschtum*, Germanness), about anti-Semitism, and so on. It was already in our minds but there was still the conflict of why we were different." If assimilation really had taken place for German Jews, then why were they still subject to anti-Semitism?

For German Jews, belief in German values was basic to their

way of life. They considered themselves to be German first and Jewish as an important second, with the exception of young urban intellectuals and those Jews of East European origins. This accounts for the very minimal interest German Jews displayed for Zionism. Those in Poland, Russia, and elsewhere were attracted to a doctrine of an independent Jewish homeland. German Jews felt at home and could not understand the need to go elsewhere. When significant numbers of East European Jews migrated to Germany in the twentieth century, they were not accepted by German Jews, who felt that their basically German values made them superior to what they considered inferior cultures. East European Jews, on the other hand, considered German Jews arrogant and essentially not Jewish enough. The animosity between these groups was intense and remains so to this day. Even now Jews of German origin sneeringly refer to Jews of East European extraction by the derogatory term "polack." In some families marriage to a Gentile is infinitely preferable to marriage to a "polack." Jews of German origin have even been accused of being anti-Semitic themselves because of their tendency to blame whatever goes wrong on "those polacks."

What are these values that German Jews believed in so passionately? The values associated with the period of the Enlightenment, such as reason and tolerance, have already been noted. The cluster of German values is often referred to as *Deutschtum,* or Germanness. Merkl's studies of German society in terms of its national character also stress such traits as militarism, authoritarianism, hero worship, romanticism, conservatism, order, and hierarchy.[13] On a personalized or individual level, German values include thrift, frugality, honesty, seriousness and simplicity. Personal lives were to be led in an orderly and disciplined fashion. The belief in order and discipline transcends to the running of society itself. The state was to be a model of efficiency. On the political level, Jews admired the same leaders as did non-Jews—men like Bismarck, Kaiser Wilhelm, and others whose politics were based on discipline, respect, and order. Germanness also included a widespread belief in the superiority of German culture—that the highest aesthetic and artistic levels were achieved in German art, music, and literature. Some Germans will argue that Goethe was a greater genius than Shakespeare and that the latter's work sounds and reads better in German than in the original English. Jews in particular admired many Jewish-German artists such as Heine, Mendelssohn, and a number of modern painters. These cultural values also included the notion that the German language was superior to others.

Among German Jews, Yiddish was despised as a corruption of the beauty of classical German; they did not speak Yiddish, deeming it the inferior language of an inferior people.

The noblest of thoughts and feelings and the very essence of everything that was good in the human species was tied to German culture. Germany contained within itself the very best of sentiments. On a more mundane level, there was the idea that Germany provided a good life for Jews, which was true even in the face of very considerable anti-Semitism. As respondents said, "Life was good, friendly and comfortable;" and when asked about the anti-Semitism they replied, "Yes, there was some of that but not enough to interfere with the good life." Perhaps Germany was indeed a culturally and socially superior country (which invented social security and old age pensions, as my respondent Mr. Abraham reminded me), but the Germans' sense of superiority sometimes extended to disdain for other Western countries, particularly the United States. Compared with Germany, the United States was a vulgar, barbaric country in the minds of many German Jews. One educated and very sophisticated professional told his American-born relative who, already in 1929, was advising emigration, "I would never emigrate to that uncivilized, barbaric country." After years of persecution and imprisonment in a concentration camp, this man was only too happy finally to arrive in the United States.

Along with these beliefs, there was naturally a strong sense of patriotism. Many Jews fought in the First World War, and in Sonderburg the names of those who lost their lives in combat are inscribed on the memorial plaque in the Jewish cemetery. This strong sense of patriotism was quickly transferred by survivors to their host country. German Jews in the United States quickly became extremely patriotic Americans, and a number volunteered for American military service. Their political allegiance was firmly centered on an intense admiration for President Franklin D. Roosevelt, whose notorious lack of interest in the "Jewish problem" was then not commonly known to the public.

Finally, along with the belief in the general social, cultural and political superiority of Germany, Germanness also included a romantic love of nature, the countryside, and particularly one's own home region. Many Jewish respondents would begin their review of the past by eulogizing the beauty of the region, "Sonderburg in the River Valley was a physical paradise." There would be glowing descriptions of the river, the hills surrounding the valley, and the picnics enjoyed in the countryside. Despite their many years in the

United States, Jews became nostalgic in their descriptions. "It was a wonderful life there, we would never have left but for Hitler," was a common refrain among them. Many of the older respondents talked about their own "no-nonsense" orderly and disciplined up-bringing, so totally unlike "how kids are brought up here without respect." In fact, the words "respect" and "decency" occurred over and over again in their conversation, harking back to the values that dominated their early years.

Because of their passionate conviction about the good society and the good life they enjoyed, many Jews had refused to believe in the seriousness of Nazism until 1938 or even 1939. Many still clung to the view that the traditional, decent, superior values of Germany, stemming from the eighteenth-century Enlightenment and the later age of modernity, would surface and the good life would return. Nazism was considered a temporary deviation from true values, despite the fact that so many of the population subscribed to it. As one elderly man noted in a letter written to his American relatives in 1937, "After all, what can they do to us, we are Germans like everybody else."

While some of these values associated with Germanness are thought to have originated during the Enlightenment, others are ascribed to the modern period beginning at about the turn of the century. Thus Merkl states that the Germans' "traditional culture began to collapse under the battering ram of historical events from the Napoleonic conquest and the popular wars of liberation to the upheaval of 1848, the national unification by Bismarck, and, most of all perhaps, the rapid industrialization and urbanization of the new nation state." The massive changes in German society as a result of modernization brought with them an emphasis on values that romanticized the past and, at the same time, attempted to cope with the changing conditions by imposing order, hierarchy, and formality on the new society. According to this view, the scape-goating of the Jews could be explained as a result of their dispro-portionate numbers in the modernizing sector of society in fields such as journalism, law, medicine, art, science and technology, business, and middlemen occupations. Jews had entered these fields rather than crafts and agriculture from which they had traditionally been excluded. Every one of these occupations "is among the chief agents of the modernization process which caused such anxiety to the inflexible people of the traditionalistic rear-guard." Seeing large numbers of competent Jews "among the harbingers of modernism, they jumped to the conclusion that the Jews were causing this frightening process of modernization."[14] Modernization and its associated values of order, hierarchy, and formality may have had some influence on the rise of anti-Semitism in Germany after 1870, and it is therefore particularly ironic to note that Jews believed in these values in much the same way as did other Germans.

But history has shown that Sonderburg Jews were not totally assimilated into the mainstream of the town and, in fact, the extent of Jewish assimilation in Germany as a whole is extremely debatable. The ease with which the forces of Nazism were able to isolate the Jews suggests that assimilation was never more than a fantasy on the part of most German Jews. Their position can perhaps best be understood by the degree to which they were structurally, culturally, and socially *integrated* into mainstream society. Two aspects of integration led some Jews to the erroneous belief that they were as German as everybody else: their participation in the institutional structures of German society, particularly their entry into high-status occupations, and their belief in and subscription to the values of Germanness. Their social marginality, however, was indicated by their exclusion from social networks, one of the more subtle and early forms of anti-Semitism. In addition, the majority defined themselves as Jews and inculcated Jewishness in their children, so that their Jewish identity kept them in a marginal position vis-à-vis the rest of society. By maintaining not only their religious affiliations but also their traditional economic institutions, they perpetuated their identity as an ethnic group and were thus perceived, categorized, and labeled as such by their Gentile neighbors. Both Jews and Gentiles observed their ethnic boundaries, reinforcing Jewish status as an observable, identifiable ethnic group. In small towns such as Sonderburg, these dynamics led to what can at best be described as a situation of stable accommodation of ethnic relations between Jews and Gentiles. Few imagined that they could be so violently disrupted.

*The author and her parents (front and left) arriving in
New York City in 1939 aboard the liner "Paris".*

8

CONCLUSION: THE MYTH OF ASSIMILATION

The rise of Nazism in Germany shocked the Jews in Sonderburg as it did Jews everywhere in the country. They found it hard to believe that after so many years of living under relatively peaceful and prosperous conditions their position or lifestyle could be threatened. In Sonderburg, the elder of the Miller family could not bring himself to leave or sell his business until 1938, although he had originally made the decision in 1936. A young professional man refused to emigrate to the United States in 1930 because he felt that nothing serious could really happen to the Jews. Mr. Martin could not persuade his mother to leave Germany in 1935 because she wanted to stay in her home town, the only community she knew and where she had lived in comfort all her life.

Elsewhere in Germany Jews displayed a similar reluctance to leave. A survivor quoted in Rothchild's *Voices from the Holocaust* notes that "I was also encouraging my parents to get out of Germany but my father thought he could only support himself in Germany and he had no money outside the country." Another survivor says that her father was told to "sell his belongings and leave the country. At the time it seemed like a disaster to part with everything and sell the business for a ridiculously small amount of money." An eloquent memoir begins as follows:

> People have asked me why the Jews of Germany, having read *Mein Kampf*, were so foolish as to stay on. Why didn't they all just leave? I tell them that if you were to tell an American Jew in Cleveland, New York, or Chicago that something might happen, very few would sell their business, very few would be willing to leave their homes and friends even to move to California. . . . They would be very unwilling to move to a different country where they would not be able to practice their professions, where they could not speak the language or make a living.

A woman remembers that her parents were talked out of going to Palestine: "What are you going to do there, they asked my father. You're still making a living. This isn't going to last. Hitler will disappear. What will you do in Palestine? Work up in the Huleh swamps and get malaria?" In his Introduction to Rothchild's book, Elie Wiesel, writing about his own town, comments that "In our town, too, we should have taken steps. Rumors had reached us; the enemy was ruthless. We could have gone into hiding, we didn't. As elsewhere, the Jews in my town refused to believe that men—Germans, even Nazis—could commit crimes so odious, so monstrous. . . . the blindness of the Jews was equaled only by the indifferences of the Allied leaders to their plight."[1]

In Sonderburg and probably elsewhere too, such disbelief was stronger among the older people. The younger ones, in their late teens and early twenties, were somewhat quicker to grasp what was likely to befall the Jews. Being younger, they thought that they could more easily create a new life elsewhere, whereas their parents had already lived more than half their adult lives in Germany. Thus, parents urged their children to emigrate "just in case," as one surviving Sonderburg Jew put it, but "we thought it would probably blow over and we could pick up the pieces again." The Kristallnacht pogrom of November 9, 1938, finally convinced doubters that the Nazis were indeed serious in their intention of destroying the Jews. The emigration figures reached their highest point in 1938 and 1939. Some people had to remain behind because they had no place to go, and still others fled from country to country in their search for safety and security.

The ambivalence German Jews displayed in trying to cope with the threat of Nazism relates primarily to their history of assimilation into mainstream German society while at the same time attempting to retain their identity as Jews. The dilemma in the 1930s of Jews threatened by annihilation is in some respects similar to the dilemma they faced earlier. Had they been willing to annihilate their own Jewishness, assuming that this would have been possible, they might have been spared the Final Solution. Some Jews did attempt, of course, to assimilate completely by converting to Christianity, but the majority of Jews wanted assimilation only if it did not require complete obliteration of their Jewishness. In fact, many strongly adhered to their Jewish identity, as did those living in the Jewish community in Frankfurt, where " 'if you were a Jew, you were bound to have strong feelings of identity, because your whole world was Jewish. Your friends, your teachers ... all ... were Jews' "[2] The small Jewish community in Sonderburg subscribed to a liberal form of Judaism rather than to Orthodoxy, and elsewhere in Germany the liberalizing movement attracted many followers. They were willing, in their drive toward assimilation, to give up parts of the religion but certainly not all of it. As Rabbi Plaut recalls in his autobiography, "we knew we were Jews and we made no bones about it. I, like thousands of others my age, tried to live in two worlds at once. I was, so to speak, a Jew at home and a German in the streets. I continued to go regularly to the synagogue; I read Jewish books. ... But otherwise my life was that of a German student who had a flair for athletics and some involvement in politics. My lack of vision was shared by the majority of my contemporaries."[3]

Even in the most assimilated families, which attended synagogue only on the important High Holidays and did not observe the traditional dietary laws, other forms of Judaism were still observed. The aspects of Judaism most crucial to the younger generation for developing a sense of ethnic identity were most strongly maintained. Thus children were given religious instruction, boys were bar mitzvahed at the age of thirteen, and important religious rituals surrounding birth, marriage, and death were followed according to Jewish laws and traditions. Above all, there was always the personal identification with being Jewish. Mr. Helfer, one of the most assimilated of the Jews in Sonderburg, belonged to several government committees and was for a time a member of the exclusionist literary society. He was respected and admired by his many Gentile friends and colleagues, who would sometimes ask him, "Why do you have to be Jewish?" "Look," he would answer, "if you had been born Jewish, you would be Jewish too." John Miller noted that "there was always a sense of being different." He also reflected the conflict involved in trying to be German and Jewish at the same time: "I don't think this whole thing was ever, from both sides, recognized. We [the Jews] felt we were on guard and we had to prove at all times that we were good Germans too. But then it would sometimes slip and when I as a little kid got beat up simply for being a Jew, the reaction was 'Ah, those Germans are bullies!' "

Jews in Germany always had to cope with the dualism of being both Jewish and German. For non-Jewish Christians, this dualism did not exist since they were simply Germans. The category "Christian German" did not exist as a type of ethnic identification. Mr. Martin noted that "we were always German Jews, they were just Germans or sometimes Christians (goyim), but never the two together." This difference is also evident, as described earlier, in the labeling of Jewish homes, businesses, and the like as Jewish, for instance, "the Jew Mandel," "that Jewish house near the railway station," "the Jewish store," and so on. It was never necessary to identify Christian German property in any other way than by referring to the family surname.

The duality of Jewish identity relates to the Jews' position, despite their acceptance, as marginal members within German society. They were caught between wanting full-scale assimilation as Germans and needing to maintain their Jewish ethnicity. This conflict was characteristic of the Jewish community probably throughout their history in Germany, but certainly most characteristic from the middle of the nineteenth century onward.[4]

As related earlier, Mrs. Miller, the wife of the richest industrialist in Sonderburg, went with her family to synagogue, sent her children to religious instruction, and identified herself as a Jew. But she also wanted membership in the restricted Casino club, and her husband apparently tried to gain it, but without success. Despite her wealth and her refined upper-class lifestyle, she was denied total acceptance into this elite level because of her Jewishness. Another survivor makes the same point in recalling her youth: " 'We were a very assimilated Jewish family although my grandparents were still observing in the Reformed way. I have fond memories of the Passover Seders at my grandfather's house, but my father did not take such things seriously. I had the usual religious instruction

... but there was no strong feeling for it. The awareness of being Jewish came because the tennis club was restricted. I belonged to a Jewish tennis club because there was no other way I could get to play.' "[5]

Thus in addition to the conflicts created by their dual allegiance, Jews also had to cope with anti-Semitism. But as noted earlier, anti-Semitism was not virulent enough to affect Jewish lifestyles in Germany and specifically in Sonderburg. As Mr. Martin said bluntly, "Sure, we had it good in Germany and all we wanted was to keep it that way. Yes, there was some anti-Semitism here, but we could still live well, if only Hitler hadn't come." A survivor from Berlin makes the same point: " 'there was a certain amount of anti-semitism; there were restrictions in universities and certain professions. Jews couldn't join the army or get any government jobs. . . . But, generally speaking, if you more or less minded your own business, you could manage well and have a pleasant and agreeable life.' "[6] Shorsch, in a definitive study of Jewish reactions to anti-Semitism, emphasizes the crucial role played by the major Jewish organization, the Zentralverein, or ZV, in mobilizing German Jewry in its fight against anti-Semitism. He notes that "the Centralverein [sic] represents a watershed in the history of emancipated Jewry. Its appearance institutionalized the twin objectives of German Jewry. Under intense pressure, German Jews served notice that they still demanded full integration into German society as well as the right to preserve their unique religious heritage." For some the Zentralverein "provided a type of surrogate Judaism." Ismar Freund writes in his memoirs that "For a large part of assimilated Jewry, the fight against anti-semitism was one of the strongest components of Jewish consciousness. To a great extent, many had emancipated themselves from the bonds of Jewish law. The national ideas of Judaism were rejected. But the will to Judaism, the Jewish feeling, existed and demanded expression. It required content. One found both in the political fight as conducted by the Centralverein."[7]

A small town like Sonderburg was somewhat remote from the mainstream of Jewish thought. Movements such as the Zentralverein were located in the major urban centers of the country—Berlin, Frankfurt, Cologne—where the majority of Jews, and particularly the intellectual leaders, lived. However, even in Sonderburg, publications of the Verein, particularly its newspaper, the *Zentralverein Zeitung,* and other Jewish publications were known to a handful of the more educated Jews. The teacher, Joshua Abraham, regularly read the newspaper and discussed its contents with his friends.

Hetta, a young girl who went to school in Frankfurt, attended Zentralverein meetings and there were others in the community who were aware of the activities of these groups and responded to them. While visiting Cologne, Hetta encountered a Zionist youth group sponsored by the Zentralverein, and this led her to emigrate to Palestine in the early 1930s—she was one of the very few Jews in Sonderburg to become a Zionist. Although the Jews in Sonderburg may not have been as directly influenced by the complexities of their ethnicity as were those in the urban centers of the country, nevertheless they too had to cope with their desire for assimilation and their need to retain their Jewishness, and to engage the specter of anti-Semitism.

Assimilation for the Jews in Germany meant several different things. In the first place, the desire of Jews to be assimilated really meant that they wanted full access to the resources and institutions of German society. They wanted, and to a considerable extent achieved, a degree of structural integration into mainstream society. In the urban areas, this included their participation in almost every occupational group. In rural areas such as Sonderburg, they were closely associated with the business, retailing, and cattle trades. All told, structural integration in terms of participating in the economic institutions of German society had developed to a very considerable point. The majority of both urban and rural Jews were middle class in terms of their socioeconomic status. In Sonderburg, for example, only three out of thirty-four families were of lower-class status and described as "poor Jews."

Second, they wanted cultural integration and this too had been achieved in both urban and rural areas. Jews participated in the cultural sectors of society—indeed, they were overrepresented in the artistic and cultural fields. Cultural integration can also be examined in terms of the value systems by which people lived. Here, Jews basically subscribed to the same set of values that characterized the overall society. These values, called *Deutschtum*, or Germanness, included pride in all things German, patriotism, the emphasis on order and discipline, love of the countryside and nature, and many other basic values (see Chapter 7). Jews and non-Jews could barely be differentiated in terms of their personal value systems. (An important exception, however, were the Jews of East European origins, who maintained to some extent the older traditional values that had evolved in Eastern Europe.)

Given this degree of institutional and cultural integration, then, it is no wonder that German Jews lived a "good life," which many of them were reluctant to leave. But they still wanted to retain their ethnicity, and this desire reinforced the anti-Semitism that had always been an undercurrent in German and other European societies from the time of the early Middle Ages. For German Jewry, acknowledgement of the "good life" was always tempered with the need to cope with anti-Semitism. This is evident from the creation of such organizations as the Zentralverein and the many others that attempted to deal with the special circumstances under which Jews in Germany lived. In day-to-day existence, anti-Semitism for many Jews was simply an accepted fact of life, but it was often not virulent enough to shatter their sense of complacency in living out the good life. In Sonderburg, anti-Semitic incidents took the form of occasional name-calling among students at school, occasional fights, and some degree of exclusionism toward Jewish students. There were also social and athletic facilities that were restricted, and there was, in addition, a latent undercurrent of anti-Semitism revealed by the common practice of labeling or identifying Jews as Jews.

Although assimilation is the term commonly applied to the position of German Jews, in actual fact, terms such as integration more closely fit their case. As long as Jews faced anti-Semitism, they were not totally assimilated into German society. But their high degree of structural and cultural integration into mainstream German society before the advent of Hitler enabled Jews to cope with anti-Semitism by accommodating. On a broader scale, German Jews created organizations to help them combat anti-Semitism; however, on a day-to-day basis, particularly in small communities like Sonderburg, Jews concentrated their priorities on living as complete a life as possible. Since they had made this accommodation, they could not readily accept the threat of Hitler and Nazism. After all, Jews had, fairly successfully, come to terms with the dilemma of their position in German society.

Even as late as the mid-1930s and afterward, Jews were still trying to accommodate not only to anti-Semitism but also to overt Nazism. Those who remained in the country still believed that the oppression would cease eventually; as Mr. Miller thought, "we could sit it out." A survivor from Mannheim remembered that "Everywhere we went there were the signs, *Juden verboten* (Jews forbidden), in the stores and the cinemas, all along the Rhine River and at all the parks and benches. The signs bothered me, but I learned to live with them. You can walk around a sign."[8] In Sonderburg, Jews also accommodated to the signs and the prohibitions by traveling out of the community as often as possible. Jews in Germany had a long history of accommodating to their position of marginality; the challenge of Nazism was yet another example of their willingness to accommodate. As Hannah Arendt notes, Jews were living in a "fool's paradise" and it was only the Kristallnacht pogrom that finally convinced them of their danger. Even the infamous Nuremberg race laws enacted in 1935 were seen as merely legalizing a de facto situation. These laws merely served to stabilize the evolving position of the Jews in Germany. By 1933 they had already been isolated from mainstream German society, and these laws only served to enshrine their isolation: "Now, the Jews felt they had received laws of their own and would no longer be outlawed. If they kept to themselves, as they had been forced to do anyhow, they would be able to live unmolested. In the words of the Reichsvertretung (Federal Representation of German Jews), the intention of the Nuremberg laws was to 'establish a level on which a bearable relationship between the German and the Jewish people became possible.' "[9]

Jews still believed that a modus vivendi with the Nazis could be achieved. Since Jews had accommodated fairly well to anti-Semitism, they tried using the same mechanism to accommodate to Nazism, since the majority of Jews and, indeed, many Gentiles believed that Hitlerism could not possibly endure in Germany. In Sonderburg, these convictions were most strongly expressed in the action of Mr. Miller, who could not bring himself to sell out and emigrate when he was still engaged in successful business with Gentile customers within the country or exporting hosiery to his foreign customers abroad. The entire experience of accommodation was neatly summed up by John Miller, after describing the many incidents that marred his youth in Sonderburg: "In Sonderburg there was no physical violence, there were no persecutions, there was a nice living aside one another. We were left alone and as a child in school there was the occasional epithet of 'Jud' and we were attacked for that maybe once or twice a year. But outside of that, I lived with my peers very well. We all lived well."

The accommodative pattern of German Jewry should not be seen as the result of cowardice, fearfulness, or economic self-interest but understood within the context of values that Jews believed in and that guided their behavior. These values, shared by Jews and non-Jews alike and associated with Germanness, emphasize in the first instance the greatness of Germany and all things German. In addition, Jews particularly emphasized those values associated with culture, education, and citizenship—or what G. Mosse refers to as

Bildung—in order to define their ethnic status.[10] These values led to a high level of integration into mainstream German society but they also influenced Jewish reaction to persecution. Accommodation is a nonconfrontive, passive, and more "cultured" reaction to persecution. One does not, therefore, picket or demonstrate against the restricted tennis club; one merely plays in another club and continues to find enjoyment in the game. In Sonderburg, Jews sometimes faced anti-Semitism prior to Hitler, but very few people confronted it in any real way. Mr. Miller attempted to use his economic power and influence so that his wife might be granted acceptance into the Women's Circle, but when his attempts failed, Mrs. Miller still cooperated with the group when they wanted to raise money for charity and needed her influence. Thus, it can be said that the Millers finally accepted and accommodated to their marginal presence within the restricted circle of Sonderburg society. Young schoolchildren sometimes directly confronted anti-Semitism by physically fighting with their tormentors, but even these incidents were sporadic. In the later period, when Nazism was being taught in the schools, Jewish children were made uncomfortable, but their only defiant act was not to give the "Heil Hitler" salute. In the small community of Hochberg, described by Dickinson, Sigmund Stein became a representative of the remaining Jewish community during the late 1930s and early 1940s, and his position clearly involved accommodating Jews to Nazism and working with Nazi officialdom. His fellow Jews in the meantime were required to work in the streets to ensure their survival, at least temporarily.[11]

It might be argued that Jews accommodated to Nazism during the 1930s because they did not have much of an alternative. For those who remained, either by choice or necessity, acceptance and accommodation meant survival for the time being at least. On the other hand, accommodating to Nazism involved a familiar response to the earlier patterns of coping with anti-Semitism. This response was deemed appropriate by German Jews and fit the model of their value system, whereas conflict or violence would have been at odds with the values that taught civility, culture, and responsible citizenship.

If the Jews had achieved an acceptable level of accommodation to living in German society, many Gentiles had also accommodated to life with Jews. With the exception of those who were always blatantly anti-Semitic, the majority of the Gentile population lived in relative stability with the Jews. In Sonderburg, this fact was often confirmed by the old Gentiles in terms of the similarities between

Jews and Gentiles; "they were just like us" or "they have always lived here" were sentiments expressed by people who wondered why Jews had been victimized during Nazism. Some said that they still did not know the reason, even after so many years had elapsed. They had been shocked and bewildered by the increasing persecution of the Jews, and one mother had explained it to her child by saying, "I don't know why—the Wolffs are Jews and we're not supposed to go there anymore." Part of the accommodation that Gentiles made had to do with the superior economic status of many Jews in their position as employers. In Sonderburg, as noted in earlier chapters, the Millers were the most important employers in the region and large numbers of Gentile families depended on them for their livelihood. Kahn's department store also employed substantial numbers of Gentiles. Thus significant numbers of Gentiles looked to the Jews in their community for their economic survival.

A mildly patronizing attitude toward the Jews was also expressed by some Sonderburgers. One old lady said that "our Jews were good people and we always got along with them." The suggestion here is that "our" refers to those who lived and were well known in Sonderburg regardless of what other Jews who lived elsewhere might have been like. But this attitude does reflect the quiet and stable accommodation Gentiles made to the Jews living in their midst.

Many Gentiles did not accept the persecution of the Jews under Nazism, but for reasons of their own, primarily because of their powerlessness, they did little to stop or influence the policies of the regime. Many went along passively and some tried in small ways to be helpful to persecuted Jews. Elie Wiesel writes that, as late as 1942–44, there were still some Germans who were trying to give aid to Jews: "even in Germany, a man here and a woman there were determined to demonstrate human solidarity with the Jewish victims. Unfortunately . . . these were exceptions."[12] In Sonderburg, too, the helpful were exceptions; but as late as July 1942, just before the last remaining Jews were deported, some of their Gentile neighbors were still bringing them food and other necessities.

The relations between Jews and Gentiles in Sonderburg and probably elsewhere in Germany before Hitler's time were described in Chapter 7 as characterized by a stable accommodation to each other's presence without any significant degree of overt or physical conflict. Following Barth again, it is worth noting by way of summary that relations between the two groups—their interethnic contact—were highly structured. There was a set of prescriptions, or rules, that regulated contact situations and that allowed people to come together in some areas of activity. For example, Gentiles could and did work for Jewish employers. Occasionally, Jews worked for Gentile employers but this occurred more often when Jews moved away from Sonderburg to larger urban centers. Rules governing contact also applied to the pedagogic sphere, where both groups attended the same schools and friendships were allowed and even encouraged. Friendships among young adults were also allowed. Similarly, relationships with neighbors were conducted with great cordiality and warmth. Gentiles routinely shopped in the stores of Jewish merchants and the customer-proprietor relationship was always close, sometimes enduring over more than a lifetime. Attendance at each other's moments of celebration for births and marriages, and even attendance at funerals was commonplace among people who knew each other well. In all of these interethnic contacts in Sonderburg, the mutually accepted rules allowed for a fairly close degree of articulation. At the same time, however, there was also a set of proscriptions that prevented interethnic contact between the two groups. The most important of these in Sonderburg (if not in urban centers of the country) was the rejection of intermarriage. Furthermore, even elite Jews were excluded from the elite social life of the non-Jewish elite. A tacit understanding also governed the ways in which both groups followed their own traditional religions, although occasionally children took part in each other's religious celebrations. And the more subtle notion that there was something different about being Jewish was recognized and accepted by both groups, and neither could bridge that difference.

Prewar German Jews and Gentiles had worked out a system that regulated their interethnic contacts. As a result, both ethnic groups could maintain their distinctiveness while living and working within the same community. Jews were thus able to retain their Jewish ethnic identity while at the same time integrating intensively into many areas of the dominant society. They were aided by their ready acceptance of German values. While this sharing in the same set of values helped them in their attempts at integration, it also intensified their dilemma of trying to be both German and Jewish. This dilemma came to a head during the 1930s when the Jews could not believe the threat to their existence in Germany. The accommodation Jews and Gentiles made to each other would, no doubt, have endured for many years had the rise of Nazism, led by a fanatical anti-Semite, not intervened to shatter their lives.

Although Sonderburg has doubled in population since the 1930s, and there is now a sprawling modern housing development, which has extended the town's borders, it is still a small, quiet, sleepy little place in which the single police station closes at noon on Friday, not to reopen until the following Monday morning. In the old section, narrow, cobblestone streets still lead off from the main street with its sturdy old homes, many of which once contained long-established Jewish families. Still there, too, are the old people who lived through the "terrible times," whose memories and thoughts were reawakened by a visiting researcher who just happened to be the granddaughter of one of the town's former Jewish families. For them, now in retirement, life in Sonderburg continues almost undisturbed. Surviving Jews in the United States are now nearing the end of their lives. Their memories and thoughts, also reawakened by the same researcher, are an ambivalent mixture of nostalgia and bitterness. Others, nonsurvivors, have had their names etched on a commemorative plaque in Sonderburg's cemetery and are remembered by the living as martyrs to an unholy cause. Some in the younger generation who left Germany as children probably think about their past and their roots on occasion, and at least one such was moved to explore and write about that past.

Appendix A

NOTES ON RESEARCH METHODOLOGY

The idea for this research project grew out of my first visit to Germany and to Sonderburg in 1975. I had for many years resisted visiting Germany since my hostility toward all things German had been with me all my adult life. As years went by, my curiosity about Germany began to overcome my resistance, and I reached a point in my life when I not only wanted but felt compelled to visit. The feeling was very similar to what Alex Haley expressed in his novel *Roots*—that one must know where one came from.[1] My initial visit to Sonderburg has already been described in the Introduction. It was after meeting Frau Kramer that the idea arose for extending this "roots" pilgrimage into a research project. I was encouraged by colleagues with whom I discussed the idea and also by my search through the anthropological and sociological literature on Germany, for I discovered that no day-to-day descriptive account of local ethnic relations between Jews and Gentiles existed. The only caveat my colleagues mentioned was that Germans would not discuss this period of history—and if they did, they would not tell the truth about their experience. But I already knew from the warmth of Frau Kramer and her neighbors' welcome that they were only too willing to talk to me. I suspect that people near the end of their lives become more willing to talk about their younger years. Besides, although I was a stranger to them, I was not an unknown entity. Several of my Sonderburg respondents admitted that they had never discussed "those terrible times,"* and for some it was a relief to do so, particularly with a sympathetic outsider who stemmed from their own community.

Rothchild, in describing the survivor interviews, states that "some survivors responded to questions as if they had been privately rehearsing the answers all the years they had been wanting to be asked."[2] Although I did not gather that impression from the Jewish survivors interviewed for this study, I did feel that way about the Gentiles. It was apparent in the way many of them eagerly discussed the subject—just as though they had been waiting for years to be asked about those times. During the years immediately after the war, they were immersed in the struggle for their own existence. Later, as Germany began its massive economic and political reconstruction, it was considered inappropriate to dwell on the past. And, of course, the shame and guilt experienced by many Germans—particularly those, as in Sonderburg, who had lived in close proximity to Jews—was something they wanted to bury and forget. It was easier to try to repress the horror than to consciously deal with it. I discovered that those who tried hardest to repress their memories were basically unsuccessful or only successful for short periods of time. The eagerness with which they now entered discussions and wanted to tell their side of the story belied their earlier attempts at repression.

Misperception due to the lapse of time no doubt entered into their discussion. For the same reason, a certain degree of distortion was perhaps inevitable in their accounts. For example, they tried to portray themselves in as good a light as possible; those who helped Jews dwelled on this aspect of their memories. Those who didn't help Jews stressed repeatedly that there was nothing they could have done under the circumstances. As described in Chapter 6, many Germans emphasized their own struggles during—but particularly

---

*The phrase or euphemism "those times" or "those terrible times" was used often by the Germans.

after—the war, implying that their turmoil was as bad as that suffered by Jews. But despite these distortions and misperceptions, my overall impression was that they were on the whole truthful.

When I returned to Sonderburg in the fall of 1980, my first call was on Frau Kramer, who again welcomed me warmly and in no time began to talk about "those times." I had, since my previous visit, been given names of several other residents with whom Jewish families had been friendly. I began to call on them one by one. In a few cases, I would telephone ahead, but with most I simply appeared on their doorsteps and introduced myself. These older persons were all retired and sure to be at home. In all instances, I was received warmly; people immediately recalled my family and the discussion got under way. I was not refused an interview by any person whom I contacted in Sonderburg. People gave me the names of other elderly residents and in that way my sample grew. The sample also grew in other interesting ways as news of my visit spread by word of mouth through this still small community, and people came forward to meet and talk with me.

For instance, during my first week in Sonderburg I was having some difficulty finding a street and I stopped an elderly lady in order to ask directions. She directed me and then asked why I was visiting "our little Sonderburg?" When I identified myself and my purpose, she looked shocked and exclaimed, "Oh, my God, you must be Willem's daughter," referring to my father who had on a few occasions treated her medically. She asked after all the members of my family and was gratified to hear that they had all done fairly well in their new country. She then said, "Oh, those times, we can't talk about them anymore, we must forget our terrible past," but immediately began discussing the thirties and particularly the deportation of old Mr. Miller. Interspersed in all her reminiscence was the phrase "we must forget the past." The ambivalence she felt was particularly evident. Despite her demur, she continued to talk about the past; the same pattern occurred in our more lengthy interview conducted the next day in her home.

One morning, within the first week of my arrival, I received a telephone call at my hotel from a woman identifying herself as Frau Bilke. She said she had known me as a child since her family home was still directly across the street from where my grandparents had lived. She said that she would love to meet me, so I visited her home that very afternoon. She explained that that morning she had met her neighbor, Frau von Himmel, who said to her (all in dialect, of course), "You can't imagine who was here yesterday—the little one from Osterman's." "But that must be Franziska," Frau Bilke replied. "That I don't know," the old lady responded. "But I know it—it must be her," Frau Bilke answered vehemently. This led Frau Bilke to phone me and, since there are only two small hotels in the town, finding me was easy. She and her husband were two of the most articulate and informed respondents.

Visitors to Sonderburg often come to "take the cure" at the mineral springs, since Sonderburg is well known as a health resort. The hotel proprietor noticed after a few days that I was not taking the cure and inquired about the purpose of my visit. When I explained it to him, his curiosity was alerted and he offered to introduce me to the old-timers who regularly came to the hotel of an evening in order to drink beer with friends. I then took to staying around the hotel and joining the tables of old men, all of whom were eager to discuss their experiences with me. One evening at dinner I happened to overhear four men in conversation at the next table. The name "Kahn," of the formerly prominent Jewish family, was mentioned several times and it became apparent that the gentlemen were discussing something from the past. I took the initiative and joined them, and it transpired that two of them had formerly been employees of the Kahn family.

The hotel contacts were extremely useful because my first round of interviews had been conducted among people who had been friendly with Jews and who had had sympathy for them. In one way or another, my initial respondents had been connected to my family whereas the persons I met at the hotel, and whom I later interviewed in their homes, were people who had no particular contact with either my family or any of the Jewish families. In several cases, though, these persons had been employed by Jews—a common pattern since two Jewish families had, between them, once employed over half of the labor force in the town.

Interviews were conducted in their homes, but the term "interview" is misleading—I rarely had to ask a question because people simply talked. Only now and then would I interrupt with a question or point of clarification; the discussions ran themselves. In most cases I took running notes, but several of the discussions were taped. Taping was of no particular advantage when the respondents used dialect, which is impossible to transcribe even for a German-speaking typist since the Rhineland, or to be more specific, the River Valley, dialect is distinctive. I transcribed and translated the taped interviews myself, which was challenging since, in some cases, the discussions lasted all afternoon or all evening, running into three or more hours. Return visits were paid to about half the sample—when I felt that certain people had more to say or when an interview had been interrupted.

An interesting problem arose during these interviews in terms of the personal way in which people responded to me. Although I carefully explained that I was a researcher and was planning to write a book, their interaction with me was based on my being a returned granddaughter of one of their families. With only one exception, no one questioned me about the research. To them my role was purely that of a returnee. Their only interest in me was that of my being Osterman's granddaughter. They couldn't care less about the research aspects of my visit. Our conversations would always begin with my family and how they were and what I knew about the other Jewish families. German respondents were pathetically eager to know that exiled Jews had done well. Usually, a person would cautiously ask me about Jewish families by beginning with a qualification such as "you don't mind me asking" or "it's really none of my business but . . . ." It was a source of relief for them to hear that Jewish survivors had done well, as though it made them feel good to know that people had prospered. One respondent put it succinctly when he said, "It relieves me to know that some of them have done well, but all those poor people who were murdered . . . ." When I said my good-byes, many people, especially the women, became very emotional and tears came to their eyes as they asked me to "remember me to so and so; come back and visit us again." My last words about the book I would write were overshadowed by promises to reach the people to whom they wanted to be remembered. The only exceptions among all of these sentimental people were Herr and Frau Bilke, both of whom were far more educated than the average resident of Sonderburg; they alone took a keen interest in the project and hoped that they would be able to read the final product.

All told, the sample consisted of thirty-one persons ranging in age from sixty-four to ninety-three, the average age of respondents being in the mid-seventies. There were eighteen women and thirteen men. All of them had known some or all of the Jewish community and about half had had friendships or work contacts with Jews. Of these, only about one-third had worked for Jews and the remainder had had either school contacts with Jewish children or casual ties such as being regular customers of Jewish merchants. Of the total respondents, four who had been civil servants had been members of the Nazi party and all of the thirteen men had been in

the German military through conscription. None had been in the
SS. No one admitted to having been a Nazi despite party membership. Of the hundred or so committed Nazis that Sonderburg had
had, not one was still alive at the time of my fieldwork. They had
been killed in the war, listed as missing on the return from the
Russian front, or had died of natural causes. When I went through
the party list with Herr Tiller, he chuckled and said, "At least they
got their return—they all died young and we are still here." This
sentiment was echoed by Minna, who said to me toward the end
of our lengthy discussion, "The funny thing is that the ones who
were the biggest Nazis are all dead. Did you know that?" She then
went through the list of names and concluded by saying, "So you
see there is a so-called *Gerechtigkeit* [justice]." A few Nazis were
said to have left the community but their present whereabouts, if
they are still alive, are unknown. Thus, unfortunately, my sample
does not include the top brass of the Nazi power structure in Sonderburg.

Because I visited Germany as the first step in this project, I was
able to collect the names of all the Jewish families who had lived
there during the twenties and thirties. The interviewing of Jewish
immigrants in the United States was expedited by this list and by
the help of a key informant, a woman who lives in New York and
keeps in touch with some of the immigrant Jews. I was therefore
able to track down each family. I would first telephone and make
an appointment to visit on some future date. These visits meant
trips to New York State and New York City, Connecticut, Massachusetts, Michigan, New Jersey, Maryland, and New Hampshire.
Several respondents lived in Florida, Arizona, and California; with
them I corresponded by mail and held telephone interviews since
budgetary restrictions prevented me from visiting them. When I
first made contact by telephone, I would state my name and give
some details about the research project. All respondents knew my
family, of course, and I was therefore not a total stranger to any of
them. Inquiries would be made about the welfare of my family, and,
although Sonderburg Jews in the United States did not maintain
contact with each other, most people knew that my father had died
some years ago. Such news is published in *Der Aufbau*—the German
Jewish paper which most still read primarily "to find out who has
died."

The interviews conducted with Jews took much the same form
as the earlier ones. As a group, they were far more interested in the
research project and several had good ideas about publication and

distribution. Some of the respondents wondered what this project had to do with anthropology, which most understood as the excavation of old bones and tools. I explained the project in terms of the discipline of ethnohistory. Their welcome was warm but not as effusive or emotional as that of the Germans. Many of the elderly Jews were especially interested to know why some of the younger generation did not become involved in that period of history. Most felt that the book would be a good thing because their suffering would be recorded and understood by younger people. Yet they still marveled that someone should be interested—since their own children were not—in what had happened in Sonderburg in 1925, and my visit gave them an opportunity to reminisce about their earlier days in that beautiful town.

In a few instances, Jewish survivors did not have the opportunity to discuss their earlier experiences in Germany with their relatives, friends or neighbors in the United States. Rothchild notes that "survivors learned to be cautious about disturbing the equanimity of friends and relations who were not prepared to cope with the harsh facts, whether they believed them or not." Some of the Jews interviewed in this study said that they had not discussed their German past with anybody in all these years. One old man described how he had attempted to tell his story to his own children, who accepted the story in its broad outlines but scoffed at some of the details. Others, like some of those in Rothchild's sample, were also "torn between remembering and forgetting, between shielding their children from their unhappy history and warning them that the world was a dangerous place.³ Perhaps my own parents also wanted to shield me from their past since, as noted in the Introduction, they had not related to me the details of their experience either. One elderly woman repeated over and over again, "Let's forget the past, that's over and done with, what good can it do to bring up all those old terrible things." But in the next breath she would revert to those very details: "Did I tell you about the time I went with some Gentile friends on a river excursion and the boat started to leak and we were all soaked? Those friends never looked me in the eye later on, but let's forget all of those things," etc. Some wanted me to meet with their children so that I could discuss this period of history with them. Apparently, none of the younger generation, having become totally Americanized, was interested in the youthful experiences of the parents.

One of the survivors in Rothchild's book also makes this point when he says, "I've been a little disappointed in my children's disinterest in my experiences in Europe. . . . My youth is so far in the past for them, so irrelevant. They are not curious. . . ."[4] And Joshua Abraham said to me, toward the end of our discussion, "I want you to meet my son. You and he knew each other as small children. Tell him what you're doing. All he wants to do is make money, he has no interest in our history. Maybe you could get him interested in these stories, but he's been a good son to us. . . ." Unfortunately, I never did get to meet his son since our paths never crossed while I was in New York.

Only two persons refused to be interviewed, and, in both cases, they were severely ill and felt that they could not withstand such a strenuous visit. Six members of the Miller family lived in a small town in Massachusetts, where I spent an entire week with them, meeting each family member on several different occasions. I had no particular contacts to this elite family since most Sonderburg Jews still maintained former social class differences. I had been told that John, the youngest brother, lived in New York, but no one could give me his address. By chance I found it in the telephone directory and simply phoned, asking the gentleman who answered if he was the John Miller of the Sonderburg family. When he replied in the affirmative, I explained myself and my mission. He expressed surprise, even shock, saying that in all these years he had never been contacted by anyone from Sonderburg. Later he told me the phone call gave him an almost mystical feeling, as though I were a voice from his past. He was extremely interested in the project and was eager to talk about his experiences in Sonderburg. I spent almost an entire day with him and his wife while he recounted, without prompting and at great length, his feelings about that period of his life. His American wife was especially interested in some of his stories, which she had evidently never heard before. The meeting with John expedited my visit to the remainder of his family in Massachusetts.

All told, nineteen Jewish survivors were traced and interviewed in this study. These persons ranged in age from sixty-three to eighty-six and, again, most people were in their seventies. As noted earlier, all had had great difficulty in resettling in the United States, but, by their middle years, most were fairly well established in occupations and living in comfortable circumstances. Their children had been born and educated in the United States, and all of them were also well settled occupationally and enjoying a typical middle-class American life.

From my point of view, the interviews in Germany were by far the more stressful. They were often very emotional for respondents, and, on many occasions, my own emotions were engaged. Simply living in Sonderburg for several months, walking the old, cobbled streets, and visiting the cemetery and the synagogue were deeply moving experiences for me. Town officials were cooperative in helping me locate archival and documentary materials on the town. One gentleman was particularly moved by the fact that a former Jewish resident would return to do this kind of project. Reading through documentary materials in the mayor's office, dry as some documents were, nevertheless proved to be an experience charged with emotion as I read about the events of 1920 or earlier in which my own grandparents—and others I had known—had participated. I came across a document in which the Jewish elders had applied for corporate (or Gemeinde) status for their Jewish community, and I saw my grandfather's signature on the petition.

Officials in Koblenz and Bad Ems, two of the archival centers for the Rhineland, were helpful in attempting to track down occupational and demographic statistics for the community during the 1930s, although this proved to be difficult since many of those records had been destroyed. Only one set of statistics for the year 1939 remained intact, and, on its folder cover, I noted that the prominently displaced Third Reich emblem—the swastika—had been exed out!

In this account I have attempted to be as objective as possible in recounting the experiences of Jews and Gentile Germans. A few readers of the manuscript have thought my treatment of the Germans too kind. I have, however, recorded events as they were told to me, and I believe that, although many Germans were passive and unhelpful to the desperate Jews, quite a number helped insofar as they could, and their aid must be recognized in an accurate portrayal of the period.

Appendix B

NOTES TO THE TEXT

Introduction

1. See Appendix A.

2. I am grateful to B. Argyle, who convinced me that this was possible.

3. Sylvia Rothchild, *Voices from the Holocaust* (Toronto: New American Library, 1981), p. 3.

4. See the bibliographies in Lucy S. Dawidowicz, *The War Against the Jews: 1933–45* (New York: Bantam Books, 1975); Raul Hilberg, *The Destruction of the European Jews* (New York: Harper and Row, 1961); Richard Hamilton, *Who Voted for Hitler* (Princeton, N.J.: Princeton University Press, 1982); and Jeremy Noakes, *The Nazi Party in Lower Saxony* (London: Oxford University Press, 1971).

5. Although there are many survivor memoirs and testimonials, I have found Rothchild's *Voices from the Holocaust* particularly useful. Material from that source is used throughout the present book for comparative purposes. Other accounts are found in D. Rabinowitz, *New Lives: Survivors of the Holocaust Living in America*, New York, Avon Press, 1977.

6. William S. Allen, *The Nazi Seizure of Power: The Experience of a Single German Town, 1930–1935*, Quadrangle Books, New York. 1965.

7. E. Labsch-Benz, *Die Jüdische Gemeinde Nonnenweier*, Wolf Mersch Verlag, Freiburg im Breisgau, 1981.

8. John K. Dickinson, *German and Jew: The Life and Death of Sigmund Stein*, Quadrangle Books, New York, 1967.

9. Martin Broszart, *Bayern in der NS-Zeit* (series on Widerstand und Verfolgung in Bayern 1933–1945. Under the auspices of the Institut für Zeitgeschichte and the Bavarian Government), R. Oldenbourg Verlag, Munich, 1977.

10. See, for example, L. Zapf, *Die Tübinger Juden*, Katzman Verlag, Tübingen; and M. Zelzer, *Weg und Schicksal der Stuttgarter Juden*, Klelt Verlag, Stuttgart, 1964.

11. Harald Luders, Director, *Now, After So Many Years*, German with English subtitles, 60 minutes, 1981. Distributed in the United States by Arthur Cantor Films, 33 West 60 St., New York, N.Y. 10023.

12. H.G. Sellenthin, *Geschichte der Juden in Berlin*, Judischen Gemeinde zu Berlin, Berlin, 1959, or any of the accounts cited in note 10 above.

13. Philip Hallie, *Lest Innocent Blood Be Shed*, Harper Colophon Books, New York, 1979.

Chapter 1

1. Historical material in this chapter is drawn from the Sonderburg archives, a local history of the community published there in 1980, and a collection of essays and articles on various aspects of Sonderburg history. The latter also includes a short article on the history of Jews in Sonderburg. Full bibliographic citations are not provided in order to protect the anonymity of the townspeople and my respondents but may be obtained from the author upon written request.

2. W.J. Cahnman, "Village and Small Town Jews in Germany: A Typological Study," *Leo Baeck Yearbook*, New York, 1947, p. 107.

3. Ibid., p. 126.

4. Ibid., p. 127.

5. Jews in Germany as a whole never constituted more than 1.9 percent (1930) of the total population between the years 1871–1933. In 1900 they were .98 percent of the population and this steadily dropped until 1933, when they were only .76 percent of the total. Sarah A. Gordon, *German Opposition to Nazi Anti-Semitic Measures Between 1933 and 1945 with Particular Reference to the Rhine-Ruhr Area*. Ph.D. Dissertation, SUNY, Buffalo, 1979, p. 413.

6. I. Shorsch, *Jewish Reactions to German Anti-Semitism, 1870–1914*. Columbia University Press, New York, 1972, p. 207.

7. The organization's full name was Zentralverein deutscher Staatsbürger jüdischen Glaubens. See Chapter 7.

8. Lucy S. Dawidowicz, *The War Against the Jews, 1933–45*, Bantam Books, New York, 1975, p. 229.

9. The total labor force was 4,757, but this figure includes workers from neighboring villages who were employed in Sonderburg. Sonderburg itself had a population of 4,357, and close to half of those employed were working class. Source: *Statistik des Deutschen Reiches*, Berlin, 1933, vol. 455.

10. Most studies that deal with social class have relied on the occupational classifications used in the German census. The difficulties inherent in this approach are discussed in Richard Hamilton, *Who Voted for Hitler* (Princeton, N.J.: Princeton University Press, 1982), especially Chapter 2. See also M.H. Kater, *The Nazi Party: A Social Profile of Members and Leaders, 1919–1945* (Cambridge: Harvard University Press, 1983).

11. K. Schleunes, *The Twisted Road to Auschwitz: Nazi Policy Toward German Jews*, University of Illinois Press, Urbana, 1970, p. 39.

Chapter 2

1. See, for example, Hans Bucheim, *Anatomy of the SS State*, (Institut für Zeitgeschichte, Munich); Walker, 1968: Heinz Höhne, *The Order of the Death's Head: The Story of Hitler's SS*, Coward-McCann, New York, 1970.

2. These figures are estimates made by both Jewish and Gentile respondents in this study. I was unable to interview any of the one hundred hard-core Nazis in Sonderburg since they had either died or moved to other areas in Germany.

3. Lucy S. Dawidowicz, *The War Against the Jews, 1933–1945*, Bantam Books, New York, 1975, p. 97.

4. William S. Allen, *The Nazi Seizure of Power: The Experiences of a Single German Town, 1930–1935*, Quadrangle Books, New York, 1965, p. 73.

5. M.H. Kater, *The Nazi Party: A Social Profile of Members and Leaders, 1919–1945*, Harvard University Press, Cambridge 1983. See also M.S. Lipset, *Political Man: The Social Bases of Politics*, Doubleday, New York, 1963.

6. Sarah A. Gordon, *German Opposition to Nazi Anti-Semitic Measures Between 1933 and 1945 with Particular Reference to the Rhine-Ruhr Area*, Ph.D. Dissertation, SUNY, Buffalo, 1979, p. 81; P. Merkl, *Political Violence under the Swastika* (Princeton, N.J.: Princeton University Press, 1965) p. 501.

7. Gordon, loc. cit., and Merkl, p. 499.

8. After the war, the American military government reviewed over one million applicants for employment in the United States zone and found that in half of them "there was no evidence of Nazi activity." Hans Rothfels,

The German Opposition to Hitler, O. Wolff, London 1962, p. 27. While this figure is probably exaggerated, it does suggest that substantial numbers of people were not actively involved with Nazism.

9.   Allen, p. 73

10.   Ibid., p. 77.

11.   Ibid., p. 136.

12.   Richard Hamilton, *Who Voted for Hitler* (Princeton, N.J.: Princeton University Press, 1982), 475–85. There were nine national legislative elections during the period of the Weimar Republic. The first of these was in 1919, and the last occurred in March of 1933 and was to be the last election held in the country, which then became a dictatorship. Throughout this period there were at least seven main parties and many smaller ones.

13.   Ibid., p. 423.

14.   Ibid., p. 598.

15.   See Hamilton, especially his bibliography to Chapter 2.

16.   Computed from Allen's table, pp. 292–93.

17.   Hamilton, p. 477.

Chapter 3

1.   As noted in Chapter 1, the Gentile population of Sonderburg contained twice as many Protestants as Catholics.

2.   See I. Shorsch, *Jewish Reactions to German Anti-Semitism, 1870–1914* (New York: Columbia University Press, 1972), pp. 144–47.

3.   K. Schleunes, *The Twisted Road to Auschwitz: Nazi Policy Toward German Jews* (Urbana: University of Illinois Press, 1970), p. 38.

4.   I am indebted to my colleague Professor E. Kallen for drawing my attention to this point.

5.   Frederick Barth, *Ethnic Groups and Boundaries,* Little, Brown, Boston, 1969, p. 16.

Chapter 4

1.   Lucy S. Dawidowicz, *The War Against the Jews, 1933–45,* Bantam Books, New York, 1975, p. 231.

2.   Ibid., p. 233.

3.   R. Thalmann and E. Feinerman, *Crystal Night, 9–10 November 1938,* Thames and Hudson, London, 1974, pp. 12–13.

4.   The organization was later to become the Reichsvereinigung der Juden in Deutschland—Federal Union of the Jews in Germany. The decree of July 4, 1939, stated that the organization was to be under the surveillance of the Ministry of the Interior, that is, the Gestapo. It began functioning under Gestapo control as early as February of that year.

5. This quotation and those in the preceding paragraph come from Dawidowicz, p. 238.

6. Thalmann and Feinerman, p. 14.

7. Source: Bruno Blau, "The Last Days of German Jewry," *IVO, Annual of Jewish Social Sciences*, vol. 8, 1953, p. 199.

8. Ibid.

9. Thalmann and Feinerman, p. 15.

10. Ibid., p. 22.

11. I. Abella and H. Troper, *None Is Too Many*, Lester and Orpen Dennys, Toronto, 1982. In an ironic footnote to history, only the Dominican Republic's dictator Trujillo was willing to accept up to 100,000 Jews. Unfortunately, this information was either not adequately communicated to the Jewish refugee organizations or Jews were perhaps unwilling to go to a country about which they knew nothing. Only 600 Jews emigrated to the Dominican Republic, and some still live there in the community of Sosua, on land donated to them by the Dominican government. B. Postal and Mistern, *A Jewish Tourist's Guide to the Caribbean*, American Airlines, 1971, p. 29. A detailed description of the Jews in Sosua is contained in my article, "The Jewish Refugee Settlement in The Dominican Republic" (in preparation).

12. Thalmann and Feinerman, pp. 22–23.

13. Ibid., p. 66.

14. See Sylvia Rothchild, *Voices from the Holocaust*, New American Library, Toronto, 1981, for many other examples testifying to the difficulties in leaving Europe.

15. Compiled from Bruno Blau, op. cit. pp. 189–90.

16. H.A. Strauss, "Jewish Emigration from Germany: Nazi Policies and Jewish Responses," Publications of the Leo Baeck Institute, New York, 1980, Yearbook, XXV, p. 327.

17. Gunther Plaut, *Unfinished Business*, Lester and Orpen Dennys, Toronto, 1981, p. 47.

18. On the disposal of properties, see John K. Dickinson, *German and Jew: The Life and Death of Sigmund Stein*, Quadrangle, New York, 1967, Chapter 2.

19. Ibid., p. 268. See Chapters 17 and 18 for an account of Stein's last days in Hochberg.

20. I am indebted to Mr. Raymond Wolff for calling this transaction to my attention and for giving me access to the archival file that contains the documents of the synagogue transaction.

Chapter 5

1. Allen, in describing Thalberg, writes that Jews there quietly accepted their new status to the point of voluntarily resigning from clubs and organizations to which they had belonged. They cited "the press of busi-

ness" and other excuses. Thus, "Thalberg's Jews were simply excluded from the community at large," and by the end of the first half-year of Hitler's regime, "the position of the Jews in Thalberg was rapidly clarified." William S. Allen, *The Nazi Seizure of Power: The Experiences of a Single German Town, 1930–1935* (New York: Quadrangle Books, 1965), 213.

2.   H.D. Leuner, *When Compassion Was a Crime*, O. Wolff, London, 1966, p. 23.

3.   Ibid., p. 102.

4.   R. Birley, Introduction to A. Leber, *Conscience in Revolt: Sixty-Four Stories of Resistance in Germany, 1933–45*, Associated Booksellers, Bridgeport, Conn., 1957.

5.   T. Prittie, *Germans Against Hitler*, Little, Brown, Boston, 1964, p. 21.

6.   R. Andreas Frierich, *Berlin Underground, 1938–45*, H. Holt, New York, 1947. See also L. Gross, *The Last Jews in Berlin*, Simon and Schuster, New York, 1982.

7.   Sarah A. Gordon, *German Opposition to Nazi Anti-Semitic Measures Between 1933 and 1945 with Particular Reference to the Rhine-Ruhr Area.* Ph.D. Dissertation, SUNY, Buffalo, 1979, p. 210. See also Gordon's Chapters 6 and 7, and Hans Rothfels, *The German Opposition to Hitler*, O. Wolff, London, 1962; M. Steinert, *Hitler's Krieg und die Deutschen*, Dusseldorf, Econ. Verlag, 1970; L. Kraushar, *Deutsche Widerstandskampfer, 1933–1945*, Berlin, Dietz Verlag, 1970; and D. Schaul, *Errinerungen deutscher Anifaschisten*, Frankfurt, A.M. Roderberg Verlag, 1973.

8.   Gordon, op cit.

9.   See U.D. Adam, *Judenpolitik im Dritten Reich*, Droste Verlag, Dusseldorf, 1972, for an analysis of all anti-Jewish laws enacted by the regime.

10.   Leuner, op cit., p. 28.

11.   The manner in which deportations were carried out varied—see, for example, John K. Dickinson, *German and Jew: The Life and Death of Sigmund Stein*, Quadrangle, New York, 1967, especially Chapter 19, for the account of the deportation in Hochberg, where the remaining Jews were removed in three successive transports. While the first two transports from Hochberg left in ignorance of where they were being sent, the last group knew that they were going to Theresianstadt—the so-called Jewish Old People's Home. Whether the Sonderburg Jews were aware of their destination is not known. According to the few accounts secured by their families later, they all died there.

Chapter 6

1.   W. Laqueur, *The Terrible Secret*, Weidenfeld and Nicolson, London, 1980, p. 17.

2.   L. Stokes, "The German People and the Destruction of the Jews,"

Central European History, vol. 6, 1973, p. 172. See also bibliographic references cited.

3. Ibid., pp. 175 and 176.

4. Ibid., pp. 181 and 182.

5. Laqueur, op cit.

6. John K. Dickinson, *German and Jew: The Life and Death of Sigmund Stein,* Quadrangle, New York, 1967, p. 275.

7. U.D. Adam, *Judenpolitik im Dritten Reich,* Droste Verlag, Dusseldorf, 1972. He makes the point that the whole Jewish issue dropped from public consciousness particularly after 1942.

8. Laqueur, p. 201.

9. For the most recent account of the callousness the Allied countries see I. Abella and H. Troper, *None Is Too Many,* Lester and Orpen Dennys, Toronto, 1982, which documents the Canadian case.

Chapter 7

1. M. Gordon, *Human Nature, Class and Ethnicity,* Oxford University Press, New York, 1978; R.A. Schermerhorn, *Comparative Ethnic Relations: A Framework for Theory and Research,* Random House, New York, 1970; M.G. Smith, *The Plural Society in the West Indies,* University of California Press, Los Angeles, 1965; Frederick Barth, ed., *Ethnic Groups and Boundaries,* Little, Brown, Boston, 1969.

2. See for example the discussion of assimilation in H.G. Adler's *The Jews in Germany* (Notre Dame, Ind.: University of Notre Dame Press, 1969), and in Eva Reichmann, *Hostages of Civilization* (Boston: Beacon, 1951), pp. 1–39.

3. Sarah A. Gordon, *German Opposition to Nazi Anti-Semitic Measures Between 1933 and 1945 with Particular Reference to the Rhine-Ruhr Area.* Ph.D. dissertation, SUNY, Buffalo, 1979, pp. 12 and 13.

4. Ibid., p. 19.

5. Ibid., p. 24.

6. Ibid., p. 23.

7. Rothchild, *Voices from the Holocaust* (Toronto: New American Library, 1981) p. 34.

8. Ibid., pp. 36–38.

9. In her fairly well known book Reichmann argues that objective differences between Jews and Gentiles greatly diminished after 1870. She states that Jewish assimilation was fairly complete between 1870 and 1933. This view fails to account for the many subtle ways in which differences were maintained by both groups. See Reichmann, pp. 1–39.

10. I. Shorsch, *Jewish Reactions to German Anti-Semitism, 1870–1914* (New York: Columbia University Press, 1972), p. 206.

11. S.M. Bolkosky, *The Distorted Image: German Jewish Perceptions of Germans and Germany, 1918–1935,* Elsevier, N.Y., 1975, p. 6.

12. Ibid., p. 13.
13. P. Merkl, *Germany: Yesterday and Today*, Oxford University Press, London, 1965, p. 39.
14. Ibid., pp. 39 and 52.

Chapter 8

1. Sylvia Rothchild, *Voices from the Holocaust* (Toronto: New American Library, 1981). These quotations are taken from pp. 35, 149, 142, 40, and 2–3 respectively.
2. Ibid., p. 38.
3. Gunther Plaut, *Unfinished Business*, Lester and Orpen Dennys, Toronto. 1981, p. 35.
4. I. Shorsch, *Jewish Reactions to German Anti-Semitism, 1870–1914* (New York: Columbia University Press, 1972).
5. Rothchild, p. 34.
6. Ibid., p. 37.
7. Shorsch, pp. 205 and 207.
8. Rothchild, p. 137.
9. Hannah Arendt, *Eichmann in Jerusalem*, Viking Press, New York, 1963, pp. 34 and 35.
10. G. Mosse, lecture given at the University of Toronto, March 20, 1983.
11. John K. Dickinson *German and Jew: The Life and Death of Sigmund Stein*, Quadrangle Books, New York, 1967, Chapters 15–18.
12. Rothchild, p. 2.

Appendix A

1. Alex Haley, *Roots*, Dell, New York, p. 19.
2. Sylvia Rothchild, *Voices from the Holocaust* (Toronto: New American Library, 1981), p. 12.
3. Ibid., pp. 9 and 10.
4. Ibid., p. 349.

Index

Frances Henry is a Professor of Anthropology at York University in Toronto. Her specialization has been in the area of race and ethnic relations. Her previous books and articles have dealt with New World Black Society with particular reference to the Caribbean and Canada. She is the author of *The Forgotten Canadians: The Blacks of Nova Scotia, The Dynamics of Racism in Toronto* among other works. Professor Henry and her family live in Toronto.